CLUELESS
IN
NEW ENGLAND

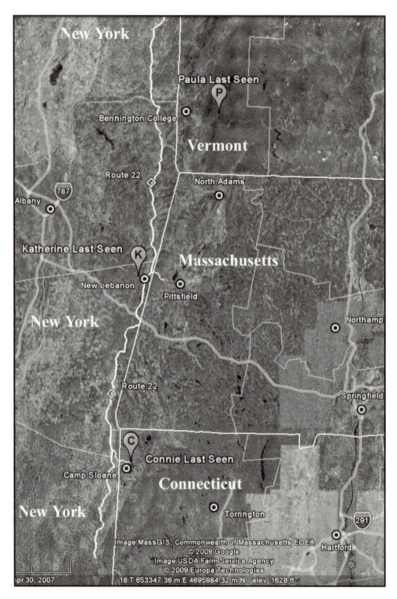

Regional Map Showing Locations of Three Disappearances
Google Earth

Clueless

in

New England

The Unsolved Disappearances
of
Paula Welden, Connie Smith & Katherine Hull

Michael C. Dooling

The Carrollton Press
MMX

Copyright ©2010 by

Michael C. Dooling

ISBN # 978-0-9627424-3-9

First Edition

No part of this book may be reproduced in any manner whatsoever including digital, electronic, photographic or mechanical means without written permission from the author and publisher, except for the use of brief quotations in critical articles and reviews.

Printed by Thomson-Shore, Inc. in the United States of America

This book is dedicated to the memory of my parents:

Detective Sergeant Edward J. Dooling
Connecticut State Police (1935 – 1955)

and

Ellen Carroll Dooling
who always loved a good mystery.

Acknowledgments

Many institutions and individuals assisted with the research for this book. Generous assistance was offered by the Connecticut, New York, Massachusetts and Vermont state police departments. They provided access to police files and participated in several beneficial discussions relating to the cases.

The *Bennington Banner* publisher Ed Woods and Executive Editor James Therrien opened their files and allowed me to reprint several photographs. The *Berkshire Eagle* in Pittsfield located the missing person circular for Katherine Hull and the *Stamford Advocate* searched their files and provided background articles. Bennington College was most generous in providing me with early photographs of the campus.

Libraries and historical societies that were particularly helpful include: Connecticut: Connecticut State Library, Ferguson Library in Stamford, Republican-American Archives in Waterbury, Salisbury Historical Society, Scoville Memorial Library in Salisbury, Stamford High School Library, Stamford Historical Society; Massachusetts: North Adams Public Library, Pittsfield Public Library, Springfield Public Library; New York: Clarkson University Library, New York State Library, Onondaga County Public Library, Onondaga Historical Association; Vermont: Bennington Free Library, Bennington Museum, Brattleboro Public Library, Crossett Library of Bennington College, Vermont State Library; Wyoming: Crook County Public Library.

Individuals who were particularly helpful include retired Connecticut state policeman Richard Chapman, Detective Karoline Keith of the Connecticut State Police, Nels J. Smith, Tyler Resch, Kristin Gibbons, Janet Rosen, Brigitte Ruthman, Alan Bisbort, Lin Maxwell, Sandy Bausch, Dr. Robert Rafford, Margaret Judith Sullivan, Dr. Albert Harper and James Scace.

Lastly but most importantly, I thank for wife Joan for her invaluable and constructive comments throughout all phases of this project.

Contents

Prologue		11
Chapter I	Woodford Hollow	15
Chapter II	The Green Mountains	81
Chapter III	Belgo Road	105
Chapter IV	West Mountain	147
Chapter V	The Hunting Ground	175
Chapter VI	Secluded Roads	201
Chapter VII	Grover's Corners	219
There's a Long, Long Trail A-Winding		223
References		225
Notes		229

Prologue

"There is nothing more dreaded than the total disappearance of an individual. When such is reported in any place, everybody thinks of its possibility within the home circle. Every case not cleared up increases nervousness as to future cases."

"Mysterious Disappearances," *Hartford Courant*, 1917

Six years apart a college student and a ten-year-old camper each went out for a walk, were seen hitchhiking for rides, and then seemingly disappeared off the face of the earth. Police and volunteers in two states searched hundreds of square miles on foot and bicycle, on horseback, by car and from the air. They found nothing. No witnesses, no shreds of clothing, no romantic involvement that would have drawn the two girls away, no domestic reasons they would have run away, no bodies…not one scintilla of evidence that would help investigators explain how they could have completely faded from existence. The two simply vanished without a trace.

Paula Welden, a sophomore at Bennington College in Vermont, disappeared in 1946 after hitchhiking a few miles off campus to walk a portion of the Long Trail. In 1952, Connie Smith walked out of her summer camp in Lakeville, Connecticut, was seen walking and hitchhiking along the road and was never seen again. The most famous cold cases in their respective states, they still remain open by the Vermont and Connecticut state police departments. These outwardly unrelated cases, occurring more than 70 miles apart, are perhaps just that – random, isolated events. Perhaps.

A person disappearing was not a new event in those days. Many other children, college students, men and women also disappeared in the Northeast during that period. Many of them ran away from home for one reason or another and returned within a short while, some did get lost in the woods or were injured and died, some moved away to escape bad relationships or to start new ones, and others decided to end their lives. A handful of them were found murdered and their killers were caught. Yet, other cases remain unsolved. Those are the ones that take on legendary proportions. In his book *Mysteries of the Missing*, Edward H. Smith wrote in 1927:

> Here we have those few and detached inexplicable affairs that neither astuteness nor diligence, time nor patience, frenzy nor faith can penetrate – the true romances, the genuine mysteries of vanishment. A man goes forth to his habitual labor and between hours he is gone from all that knew him, all that was familiar. There is a gap in the environment and many lives are affected, nearly or remotely. No one knows the why or where or how of his going and all the power of men and materials is hopelessly expended. Years pass and these tales of puzzlement become legends. They are then things to brood about before the fire, when the moving mind is touched by the inner mysteriousness of life.[1]

The Welden/Smith disappearances fall into just such a legendary class. Neither Paula nor Connie ever returned home, their bodies were never found, and no solid clues were uncovered. Nothing held any promise in explaining the facts in the cases – nothing to indicate the fates of the two unfortunates.

But another disappearance a few years earlier, midway between the sites where Paula Welden and Connie Smith were last seen, has striking similarities to the other two cases. A stenographer from

CLUELESS IN NEW ENGLAND

Syracuse, while visiting her grandmother in New York's Lebanon Valley along the New York/Massachusetts border, decided to go for a walk and was later seen hitchhiking. And she too was never seen again . . . that is, until more than seven years later, when a hunter came face to face with her skull perched in the crotch of a tree on a mountainside outside of Pittsfield, Massachusetts. Investigators concluded that Katherine Hull must have become lost in the woods, gotten injured and perhaps died of exposure. There were no clear answers for her family as to what had actually happened to the young woman. Once her identity was established, the case was officially closed.

The three unsolved disappearances, falling almost in a straight line north to south, are unsettling to say the least. Despite the Herculean efforts of law enforcement agencies and hundreds of volunteers who searched for the missing women, no clues were identified that would lead the investigators to any solutions. In a strange way, it is the complete lack of clues and the failure to attain any satisfactory resolution of these three disappearances that seems to draw them together. Looking back on these cases with 21st-century eyes, with what we know of the behavior of serial killers and the patterns they follow, perhaps these cases aren't so mysterious after all.

Chapter I

"Once is happenstance..."

Ian Fleming, *Goldfinger*

Paula Welden
Courtesy of the Bennington Banner

CLUELESS IN NEW ENGLAND

Woodford Hollow

Innocence

Independent...that's the best way to describe Vermont. The state's spirit of independence dates back a long time. In the 18th century, a conflict arose between New Hampshire and New York as to who controlled the land between those two states. The king of England had declared New Hampshire's rights were invalid and the Vermont lands belonged to New York. Military action was undertaken by Vermonters in the form of The Green Mountain Boys. Ethan Allen, whose home and iron forge were in Salisbury, Connecticut, was selected to lead the group. The small band of volunteers raised havoc with the New York settlers, captured Fort Ticonderoga in 1775, and was later involved in the defeat of General Burgoyne at the Battle of Bennington in 1777. A monument built to commemorate this important battle is one of Bennington, Vermont's chief landmarks. The land ownership conflict was further complicated by the outbreak of the American Revolution. Vermont's solution? It declared itself an independent commonwealth in 1777 and remained so until 1791, when it was admitted to the Union.

That same spirit of independence continued as Vermont matured. It shows up in legislation, such as laws relating to civil unions, and in less personal areas, including the banning of billboards from their highways in 1945. The town of Bennington, in southern Vermont, was one of the first communities to impose the ban of billboards that "hide the everlasting hills with blatant hyperbole in letters ten feet high."[2] Earlier, Bennington had taken the bold step of adopting Daylight Savings Time years before any other town in Vermont.[3] During that time of year, Vermonters and visitors would have to re-set their watches as they traveled in and out of Bennington.

Bennington is idyllically situated between the Taconic Mountain Range and the Green Mountains. Two valleys converge there – the Valley of Vermont to the north and south, and the Walloomsac Valley to the west, carved by the river of the same name. To the east is the southern portion of the Green Mountains that extend into Canada. To the northeast is the first high peak in that range, Mount Glastenbury, rising over 3,700 feet. It is only a few hundred feet lower than Vermont's highest point, Mount Mansfield, near the Canadian border. In 1946, Bennington was home to about half of the 23,000 residents of mountainous Bennington County.

Monuments and mountains are not Bennington's only high points. It is also graced with a distinctive institution of higher learning, Bennington College, which is located about four miles north of the center of town. The entrance to the college is on Route 67A and has a long driveway leading up to the campus that is situated on some 470 acres. In 1946, as much of it still is today, the campus was laid out as a New England village. The student houses were arranged around a central green at the head of which is The Commons building that housed the post office, the cooperative store, theatre, infirmary and the dining rooms. The original dormitories were large New England-style, white clapboard-sided houses and could accommodate about twenty-five girls each. Besides a mixture of single and double rooms, the student houses had a living room, kitchen and laundry. There were about 300 women enrolled in the college in 1946, and they had been selected, not based on grades or admission tests, but on their interest in learning and the promise they showed in their fields of study.

Bennington College was a relative newcomer to Vermont, having opened in 1932. Founded as an alternative to the traditional women's college, it focused on the development of the individual student's needs and interests. The students were very much active participants in planning their courses of study. The *College Bulletin* described the experience, "The students are allowed to impose their own disciplines. Students, as they advance, find themselves in the same relation to their fields as is any adult worker: the subject is never exhausted, and there is always work to be done."[4] The central philosophy of the college was that "Bennington students should themselves find a useful field in which to work, that emphasis should be on the development of initiative, on self expression, on creation rather than imitation, and on independence of mind and body...A girl may substitute murals for a graduation thesis, or she may design a house for credit. Perhaps she will print a book, or do a long series of wood cuts. Anything counts which has meaning."[5] The curriculum was designed around the individual student's interests and alpha-numeric grades didn't exist. Instead, a student's performance was summarized in detailed descriptive reports by the instructors twice a semester. A first-year student was only invited back if she demonstrated progress in her field of study and had adapted to the independent philosophy of the school.

One such student was Paula Jean Welden, who had completed her first year at Bennington and had been invited back for the 1946-1947 school year. Paula lived in Stamford, Connecticut and was the daughter of Mr. and Mrs. William Archibald Welden. She was born on October 19, 1928, in Bronxville, New York, and the family moved to Brookdale Road in Stamford when she was seven months old. Her father was born in Scotland and was an industrial designer with Revere Copper and Brass Company. Her mother Jean was listed as a homemaker in the 1930 census, when Paula was just $1^1/_2$ years old. Paula had three other sisters – Pamela (age 16 and a student at Stamford High School), Stephanie (age 14) and Heather (age 5), both students at Willard Elementary School in Stamford.

Michael C. Dooling

Paula graduated from Stamford High School in 1945. Although unquestionably an attractive young woman and once described as a "patrician beauty," her high school friends nicknamed her with the masculine "Paul." Paula was active in several Stamford High clubs and activities including the Classical League, Le Circle Francais, Yearbook Art Committee, the Debating Club, and the Stamford Hospital Art Project in which she helped paint murals in the children's ward. The quote appearing next to her photo in her yearbook reads, "The friends who are most stimulating to us are those who disagree with us."[6] She also mentioned her plans for the future next to her photograph – "Future – College, Art School."

At Bennington College, Paula was a resident of Dewey House where she roomed with Elizabeth Johnson of Putney, Vermont. The two had roomed together during freshman year and continued to do so during their sophomore year. Many students worked various jobs on campus to offset the $1,850 tuition, room, and board though most earned no more than $250 in an academic year. Paula and Elizabeth were no exceptions; both worked in the dining hall on campus, normally from 8:20 A.M. to 9:30 A.M. for breakfast and 12:20 P.M. to 1:30 P.M. for lunch.

At the beginning of her freshman year, Paula thought she had known exactly what she wanted to become – an artist. Her father was a talented industrial designer and she intended to follow his creative lead in her own career. As her freshman year passed, however, she became less and less confident that art was her future. It appears to have bothered her that the direction she had headed for her entire life was now in question. Her roommate wrote, "Paula was very sure of herself when she first came to college. She knew just exactly what she was going to get out of college and what she was going to be. She was going to be an artist, and a good one. She was pretty sure what good art was, and what a good artist should do. Everything Paula did or saw was going to help her in her art in some manner."[7] But she didn't like her first art class, finding it too elementary, and she questioned the abilities of the teacher in her second class. Her heart didn't seem to be in art any longer and other interests started to gain her attention.

Paula found herself drawn to music and even more to botany. Elizabeth continued, "On the field trips she was always the first to learn the names of the plants and the one who found the rare plants. After such a field trip and especially after she had found a beautiful rare flower, Paula would come into our room dancing with delight and happiness. Paula loved beautiful things. After every Botany class she would be gay and happy and enthusiastic. She would tell me with tremendous delight what she had seen on her field hikes."[8] She would get equally excited about what she could see with the aid of a microscope and intended to bring all she observed in botany into her own art.

Paula and Elizabeth immediately hit it off when they met as freshmen and became close friends. Elizabeth had a much different upbringing than Paula; Elizabeth grew up on a ranch where her family raised horses. An "outdoorsy" girl, she enjoyed horseback riding, hiking, tree-climbing and camping. Paula wasn't acquainted with many of these pursuits, though she quickly learned to enjoy them when Elizabeth introduced her to them.

As opportunities for hiking and camping presented themselves, Elizabeth and Paula seized them. Two of Elizabeth's cousins invited them to climb Mount Equinox near Manchester, Vermont, one of the highest mountains in the southern part of the state. Rather than take the trails to the top of Equinox, the four decided to bushwhack their way upward. Though a tiring hike, Paula thought it was "marvelous fun."[9] Not long after that, two friends from Williams College, Allan Schauffler and Denny Volkmann, asked them to go hiking, camping and square dancing. Skipping the big fall dance being held at Bennington College that weekend, the four, joined by several others, hiked mountains near Mount Equinox. At the end of the day, they ate supper in the rain after which they went to a square dance at the Manchester Grange. Since it was still raining, and camping would be miserable, a farmer they met offered to let them all sleep in his hay barn. A few weeks later, they hiked and stayed overnight on Pine Cobble Mountain, which looks down on Williams College. Inspired by their hiking experiences, Paula and Elizabeth wanted to explore more of the mountains and trails that surrounded Bennington. One of the more popular trails in Vermont - the Long Trail - was relatively close to the college but the two roommates hadn't yet had the opportunity to hike it.

Paula and Elizabeth found their adventures in the mountains to be therapeutic. Elizabeth reflected, "These trips into the hills were wonderfully refreshing and envigorating (sic) like nothing else. After such a trip we could put a lot of fresh energy into our studying. Our minds worked quickly and all the tiredness of a week's steady grinding was pretty nearly gone. The difference in our mental state of mind and our ability to study well, on weekends when we stayed working and when we got outdoors to play, was tremendous."[10] Elizabeth was shocked later on when people implied romantic reasons for their mountain excursions. "...it has been pointed out to me that these trips look as if they were specially designed for love making. I have astonished many people by saying such an idea never occurred to me or to Paula. We went out for exercise and fresh air and hiking with boys is just that much more fun. To Putneyites it is a very ordinary thing for groups of boys and girls to hike and camp out together. Love making is not part of it. It is a thing more like boys and girls square dancing, singing or working together."[11]

Elizabeth also introduced Paula to square dancing and she fell in love with it, becoming quite accomplished at it. They used to get together with the "kitchen boys" who worked as cooks in the campus dining hall and would go to various dances. There was no pairing off of couples and the nature of the dance involved constant switching of partners.

There did not appear to be any single young man to whom Paula was romantically attached. Through friends, she had gotten to know some men from Williams College in North Adams, Massachusetts. She attended two formals at Williams College, one with a logic student named Don. Paula and Don had several dates but their relationship didn't develop into anything serious. On another occasion, Paula went to a formal at Yale University and spent the evening with a boy whom she knew from high school. Things went fine at first but according to her roommate, toward the end of the dance, her date started getting "pancakey." "When boys started getting that way, Paula always wanted to flee. It gave her the creeps."[12]

On several occasions, Paula went to Putney to visit with Elizabeth's family and to socialize at the Putney School where Elizabeth had attended high school. There, Paula had her first experience riding horses, an activity she thoroughly enjoyed. One weekend the two attended the Putney School Harvest Festival, a country fair with oxen-pulls, horse-riding competitions, square dances, and prizes for cooking, livestock and vegetables. Paula and Elizabeth participated in a corn-husking contest and to everyone's surprise, Paula won. Elizabeth recollected, "The biggest surprise of Paula's winning the corn husking contest was the prize. It was a great grey goose, and Paula nearly exploded with laughter at the sight of it. She paraded around the rest of the day with the goose under her arm. What a surprise it would be for her family!"[13]

Several times, Paula invited her roommate to her family home in Stamford. Paula seemed to have a tenuous relationship with her parents, describing her house to Elizabeth as an "ice box." Elizabeth didn't see Paula's parents as being cold. If anything, the coolness seemed to be more on the part of Paula. When her father asked her about college life, Paula became irritated and was reluctant to offer much information. It was as if she didn't know him, yet she always spoke very highly of him and his accomplishments to her roommate. She had been very close to her mother before going off to college but hadn't had a heart-to-heart talk with her since she left. Paula had several concerns about telling her parents too much and may have wanted to avoid a possible conflict over her change in interest from art to botany. She hadn't written home much lately and had taken a couple of courses they didn't approve of – dance, which she had dropped, and music. The Weldens didn't feel Paula was getting the best art training at Bennington, and Paula had serious doubts about the quality of the training herself and whether she even wanted to continue to major in it. Also, Paula didn't feel she was becoming the talented artist her father had hoped she would be. Elizabeth noted, "So Paula was feeling a little hurt, a little guilty, misunderstood, and a little frightened when she arrived home."[14]

Perhaps in part due to her friendship with Elizabeth, Paula had developed an element of fearlessness. For example, when Elizabeth took Paula to Putney for the weekend, they usually hitchhiked there - a distance of more than fifty miles. Elizabeth wrote, "Paula did not mind hitchhiking. In fact, it was more fun than going by bus as you met all kinds of interesting people."[15] On another occasion, at the end of her freshman year, Paula expressed concern about how to ship her bicycle home. Her roommate said jokingly, "Why not ride it home?"[16] Paula took her suggestion seriously and decided to exercise her own independence. She started to ride her bike frequently so she could build up her strength and surprisingly, she convinced her parents to let her ride her bike home to Stamford, some 165 miles distant. Elizabeth reflected on the event, "Well, summer came and I mounted the train and she mounted her bike, and we headed for opposite ends of the country. We wrote each other once that summer, and Paula's letter told of her trip home through rain and muck. She said how nice everyone had been to her as she biked through, and she had really had a marvelous time despite the bad weather. The trip gave her a good, free and independent feeling."[17]

The weekend before Thanksgiving in 1946, Elizabeth had gone home to Putney by herself, which seemed to have a negative impact on Paula. When she returned, she found Paula to be gloomy, restless and moody. Paula had spent a boring weekend, mostly by herself, and it dawned on her just how dependent she was on one person for her social life and it was bothering her. The two girls talked about it, and they agreed they should both expand their circle of friends. Paula still seemed restless to her roommate that week, appeared distracted and distant, and she slept more than usual. At times, Paula stared out the window, paced the floor, sat on her bed strumming her guitar and a few times fell asleep with her clothes on.

Thursday, November 28th was Thanksgiving Day. Unlike American campuses today, Bennington College closed for only the holiday itself; and classes were held the day after. Many Bennington College students didn't bother going home for the one-day holiday. Paula's mother had sent her a check to cover her transportation costs, but she didn't want to go home because of the cold, strained atmosphere there. On the other hand, she didn't want to stay at the college on the holiday either. After vacillating for several days, she decided not to make the trek to Stamford and back. She told her parents that she could not go home because something had come up.

There was the promise of an interesting weekend if Paula stayed in Bennington. First, she had a date for a square dance that weekend and second, while waiting tables in the dining hall two girls invited Paula and Elizabeth to join them on a hike up the Long Trail on Thanksgiving Day. Paula was excited about the prospect of that hike even though Elizabeth was going home for the holiday.

Unfortunately for Paula, the plans fell apart when the two girls decided to go home for Thanksgiving.

On the evening before Thanksgiving Day, Paula went to the movies with freshman Ursula Keller. Paula apparently had decided to do something about her dependence on her roommate for companionship. Her reliance on her roommate was generally known and several students had noticed her efforts at developing new friendships. The two had a good time and Ursula described Paula as being quite talkative. After they returned to Dewey House, they chatted, primarily about religion and boys. Ursula tried to engage Paula in a serious conversation about religion, but Paula was especially interested in talking about the opposite sex.

On Thanksgiving evening, Paula attended a square dance at the college. She had attended other square dances in the area and at one the previous school year had met a young man, Harold Colvin, whose brother Russell worked in the kitchen at the college. Their paths crossed again at another square dance in the fall and Russell had arranged a date for his brother Harold with Paula for the Thanksgiving night dance. Russell had been asked to the dance by Bennington College student Elizabeth Olsen. The four attended the dance in the carriage barn at the college and spent the entire evening together. After the dance, they played billiards for a while on the upper level of the barn. Harold and Paula talked about a possible date the following week and he promised to call her early in the week to set it up. At the end of the evening Harold walked Paula back to Dewey House and said goodnight, making no attempt to kiss her. They left on good terms and Harold thought she behaved as she normally did throughout the evening. Their relationship was purely social and there was no apparent romantic involvement.

Elizabeth returned from Putney early Friday morning in time for her classes. She and Paula spoke only briefly and Elizabeth left for class. That evening, Elizabeth was studying and didn't pay much attention to her roommate, though noticed she appeared restless. They went to bed about 11:00 P.M. and both slept late on Saturday morning. Elizabeth awoke with a start and tried to wake up Paula. She pretended to be asleep as Elizabeth mockingly threatened her. Paula giggled and Elizabeth tipped her bed over, dumping Paula on the floor. Both had a good laugh and left for their morning shift at the dining hall in great spirits.

Dewey House
Courtesy of Bennington College

Much of Paula's work for the semester was completed. She had passed her Music test, completed her Cultural Anthropology paper and had no end of semester tests or projects for Art. She only had a Botany test and she knew the material pretty well. Elizabeth had several papers due and tests to study for and spent much of Saturday and the following day writing and studying. Elizabeth was still studying Saturday evening and described Paula as being "very restless and full of life and energy."[18] Paula joined a group of girls in the living room of Dewey House, where they started "Indian wrestling" and became very noisy. Paula was right in the middle of things and at one point went back to her room to get Elizabeth to show the girls "how it was really done." Elizabeth obligingly went downstairs and joined the roughhousing until girls in the rooms upstairs complained they were "making absolute thunder and the house was shaking."[19] It was into the quiet hours, and Paula and Elizabeth went to their room and to bed.

All seemed normal in Paula's life as she turned out the light that night. This was not to say everything was perfect. She had her uncertainties about her college course of study and friendships. Like most college students in this regard, Paula had started to sort out her personal interests from her parents' wishes, begun to expand her circle of friendships at the college, and was beginning to exercise her own independence. She was perhaps a bit reticent when it came to boys but had become involved in co-ed group activities such as square dancing and hiking. Her life at Bennington College was not unlike that of any other college girl. Any self-doubts, lack of confidence, and desires for close friendships seemed to be simply part of the maturation process and she didn't appear to suffer from them any more than most young women her age.

Alarm

On Sunday morning, the sky was gray and a few snow flurries speckled the landscape. Neither Paula nor her roommate talked much and, during the morning work shift, they perfunctorily waited on their tables. Paula had woken up "sort of gloomy"[20] and Elizabeth encouraged her to lift her spirits by going for walk after lunch, but Paula was non-committal. Later that morning, December 1st, Paula donned a green smock to work the lunch shift at The Commons, a short walk from Dewey House. Another student had asked her to work as her substitute at the noon meal for that weekend. Paula agreed to do it and had worked Thanksgiving Day for her as well. During the lunch shift, Elizabeth asked Paula if she was going for a walk, hoping that another girl might hear her and offer to join her. Though there were some expressions of interest, no one seemed to have the time.

The Commons at Bennington College
Courtesy of Bennington College

After Paula finished working her shift, she ate lunch, returned to her room, changed into blue jeans and thick-soled sneakers, and donned a red parka with a fur-trimmed hood. Her roommate hadn't returned yet because she had to stay to clean the faculty dining room. Elizabeth finished her shift at 2:30 P.M. and when she arrived at their room Paula wasn't there. She assumed Paula had gone for a walk after all.

Perhaps to energize herself and improve her state of mind, as hiking had done for her in the past, Paula left Dewey House between 2:30 P.M. and 2:45 P.M., and proceeded down the driveway toward the entrance to the college. A car passed her going in the same direction. Two former Bennington College students, Patricia Beck and Mary Watson Fruitrich, were in the car; they slowed down, waved and proceeded on their way. Paula knew Patricia and Mary from the previous year when they had lived in Dewey House though they had since graduated. Paula waved back and smiled. The girls didn't think to stop and offer her a ride because it appeared to them, by the way she was dressed, that she was just out for a walk. When Paula left her dormitory, the weather was pleasant and the temperature was in the forties. She dressed appropriately for the weather conditions that afternoon, but not for that evening; either she was not planning to be out late or she did not know that the weather was forecasted to worsen. That night, the temperature dropped some forty degrees to five above zero, and later it started to snow.[21]

When Paula didn't return by dinner time, Elizabeth became concerned. At bedtime, Elizabeth thought Paula's absence strange and speculated to herself that she might have gone to study in the science building, where it was quieter. Elizabeth drifted off to sleep, expecting her to come in any moment. When she awoke the next morning, Elizabeth jumped out of bed and yelled for Paula to wake up; she had slept late again. It quickly became apparent that Paula had not returned. She rushed to the dining hall and asked the head waitress if Paula had called in the night before to arrange for a substitute. She had not. Elizabeth then checked the infirmary, only to learn she wasn't there. Elizabeth had to get to her job in the dining hall for breakfast and immediately after finishing went to the House Chairman's office. The two of them searched several buildings and when they found no sign of Paula, they contacted the Director of Admissions.

When she left Dewey House the previous afternoon, Paula probably had no more than ten dollars on her and she left an uncashed check for another ten dollars in her room. Neither her clothing, nor the amount of money she had with her, gave any indication she intended to stay away longer than a few hours. Students were required to sign out with the campus switchboard if they intended to return to campus after 11:00 P.M. and to sign in with the security officer when they returned. The signing out process was for security and courtesy purposes, and there were no restrictions regarding the number of evenings a student could spend off-campus or the time by which they needed to return. In the morning, an appointed student was responsible for checking on the presence of every student in the house. If Paula intended to leave the college permanently without being discovered for several days, all she needed to do was sign out that she would be returning after 11:00 P.M. or that she would be gone for several days. By not signing out beforehand and not returning to campus before 11:00 P.M., Paula set in motion an alert on campus.

When Paula didn't attend her classes on Monday morning, the Director of Admissions, Mrs. Mary Garrett, contacted the college president, Lewis Webster Jones, to report a missing student. Around 1:00 P.M. she contacted law enforcement authorities. Garrett contacted William Travers Jerome, Bennington County's State's Attorney. Jerome was a graduate of Yale and Columbia Law School and a distant cousin of Winston Churchill. In 1946, each of

Vermont's fourteen counties had an elected sheriff who was responsible for county-wide law enforcement services. Each sheriff, including Bennington County's W. Clyde Peck, reported to the county state's attorney. There was no state police organization at the time and the Department of Motor Vehicles patrolled roads and investigated traffic accidents while the county sheriff, state's attorney, and a state investigator were responsible for criminal investigations.

School officials contacted Paula's family on Monday morning, cryptically inquiring about Paula and hoping she had gone home for some reason. She had not. That afternoon Mr. Welden took a train from Stamford to Bennington. Paula's mother stayed behind with her other three daughters and anxiously waited by the telephone for a positive word. When asked by a reporter about her daughter's disappearance, Mrs. Welden said, "She's always been a good student and had excellent marks,"[22] and discounted the possibility that Paula went off with some boyfriend. Mrs. Welden said she had no partiality to any particular boy.

On Monday afternoon, investigators made calls to hospitals in Vermont and New York inquiring if Paula had been admitted. The state police in New York were notified to keep watch for her. The campus buildings and grounds were searched Monday afternoon. Students in her botany class remembered Paula had once expressed interest in hiking to Everett's Cave. A group of students, accompanied by their instructor Robert H. Woodworth, hiked to the cave on Mount Anthony southwest of Bennington center, and searched the area. They found no trace of Paula. Meanwhile, the state's attorney issued a missing person bulletin with a physical description of Paula to police departments and newspapers.

College officials, the sheriff and local police began to investigate her disappearance, interviewing witnesses and constructing a timeline of events. As the investigation progressed, the sequence of

Paula's actions after she left her dormitory started to emerge. Shortly after she left the safety of the campus, Paula was seen walking along the road by Danny Fager, who operated Shantley's gas station near the college entrance. He watched a girl wearing a red parka and blue overalls walk up a pine tree-covered knoll near the entrance, run down the knoll to the road, and then head toward the center of Bennington walking along Route 67A.

Around 4:00 P.M. Paula was seen by Ernie Whitman, a night watchman at the *Bennington Evening Banner* newspaper office. Whitman and three friends – Stearns Rice, Mary Rice and Lyman Royce – had spent the day at their camp on Bickford Hollow Road. Ernie Whitman and Mary Rice were ahead of the others as they walked down the Long Trail toward their car. A young woman resembling Paula Welden asked them for directions to the Long Trail, saying she wanted to hike it. According to Mary Rice,[23] the girl resembling Paula asked, "Is this the Long Trail?" After they told her it was, she asked, "Does it go on over the mountain?" She also asked them how far the trail went. Ernie told her he had only traveled five miles of it but it went all the way to Canada. The young woman thanked him and, even though it was approaching dusk, proceeded across a bridge that only led to the Long Trail. They noticed she had blonde hair and was wearing a red jacket.

The Long Trail starts at the Massachusetts border of Vermont and runs the entire length of the state up to the Canadian border. It hugs the main ridge of the Green Mountains and is the oldest long distance trail in the United States. Built between 1910 and 1930, it was partly the impetus behind the creation of the Appalachian Trail. The two trails are one and the same for about 100 miles in southern Vermont. The Long Trail is 270 miles long and crosses the highest peaks in the Green Mountain range. Along the trail were some fifty-seven cabins and 100 lean-to shelters, many of which were equipped with food and fuel supplies.

When the story of Paula's disappearance went to press on Tuesday, Ernie Whitman was cleaning the floor in the pressroom. He saw the headlines and Welden's photograph on the front page and informed reporter Pete Stevenson that he had seen and spoken to the missing girl. Paula's father was present at the time and wanted to start searching immediately. It was 5:30 in the afternoon and already dark. Nevertheless, Welden, Stevenson and Frank Howe, the *Banner's* editor, left for Woodford Hollow. They interviewed several residents there and three of them said they had seen a young woman answering Paula's description heading toward the Long Trail. One resident said he had seen her on the trail near a camp named Hunter's Rest.

The three searchers started up the Long Trail armed with flashlights. They searched a twenty-foot swath on both sides of the Long Trail. Walking was hindered by snow that had fallen on Sunday night. They progressed to a camp owned by William Lauzon who told them he hadn't seen the girl. Lauzon did tell them that three servicemen had stopped at his camp on Sunday around noon and asked him to hold a suitcase for them. They continued up the Long Trail toward a camp owned by a Mr. Sausville even though they weren't particularly dressed or equipped for a long hike. The two sailors and one soldier hadn't returned as of that Tuesday night.

Upon opening the suitcase the men found government-issued clothing with laundry markings indicating ownership by J. W. Carrol, William Watts and M. Golder. They also found a letter written to one of them from an address in Nichols, New York. One of the *Banner* reporters contacted a high school principal in that town who put him in contact with the woman who wrote the letter to J. W. Carrol. She informed the reporter that Carrol was in the navy and had once lived in Vermont. The three men were later picked up and questioned for five hours by the state's attorney, the Bennington College president, Sheriff W. Clyde Peck, and Deputy Sheriff Leroy

Dunn. They determined the three had no connection to the Welden affair and were released. Investigators were no more enlightened than when they started.

A building contractor stepped forward on Wednesday with information about Paula's journey toward the Long Trail. Louis ("Deke") Knapp was driving home and saw Paula thumbing along Route 67A. He stopped and picked her up about 400 feet east of the college gate around 3:00 P.M. He was pretty certain about the time and his wife confirmed that he came home around 3:15 P.M., a few minutes late for their Sunday dinner that she usually served at 3:00 P.M. Knapp was driving an International pick-up truck and Paula slipped on the running board when she got in, and he told her to watch her step. The girl asked him, "If by chance you are going out Route 9, I would like to ride out with you."[24] She said she wanted to go to the entrance to the Long Trail. Knapp told her he lived down that way and gave Paula a ride as far as his home on Woodford Road. Although they didn't converse much during the drive, "the girl acted in a cheerful manner during the whole trip."[25] Knapp dropped her off and Paula said, "That's swell. Thanks a lot."[26] He last saw her walking in the direction of the Long Trail, which at that point was still about three miles away.

When Louis Knapp saw the article in Tuesday's newspaper, which he read Wednesday night, he realized the girl he had driven on Sunday was missing and contacted authorities at Bennington College. He described Paula as "wearing a jacket, color brown with a hood hanging down the back. She was wearing a pair of overalls, color blue. She had light brown hair."[27] The discrepancy in jacket color was perplexing since he was in such close proximity to her and spent a relatively long time with her. It was later resolved when it was determined that Knapp was color blind, a condition he had not been aware of before he gave his statement.

It seems a large number of people noticed Paula Welden's final journey to Woodford Hollow. Shortly after Knapp dropped Paula off on Route 9, Cora Mallory and her son Edward Welch, who lived along the same road, saw a girl matching Paula's description thumbing for a ride heading east toward the Long Trail. Edward thought the girl was someone else at first and went out to greet her. He then realized it wasn't who he thought it was. Cora's daughter, Evelyn Harwood, lived two doors down and saw a girl dressed like Paula walking in the same direction at a fast pace and trying to get a ride from passing cars. She noticed the girl because she too mistook her for someone she thought she knew. Mrs. Harwood determined the time to be about 3:30 in the afternoon as the latest episode of the long-running radio serial *One Man's Family* had just started.

Paula was then seen by Mrs. Archie Barbeau whose house was on Route 9 near the entrance to the Long Trail about $^6/_{10}$ mile east of the Harwood home. The girl stopped briefly by her mail box and proceeded on. Mrs. Barbeau believed the girl wore a red jacket, a red tam and pants that appeared green. She noted the time on her watch was 4:00 P.M. but told investigators her watch ran twenty minutes fast, placing Paula there about 3:40 P.M. Mr. Barbeau reported that the morning after Paula disappeared there were footprints in the snow in back of his house on the Long Trail. They showed that someone had walked in for a few hundred feet, turned around, and returned to the road.

Rose Michaels, an attorney in Bennington, owned the last camp on the road portion of the Long Trail a short distance above the Fay Fuller camp, a Boy Scout lodging constructed of stone. The day before Paula's disappearance she noticed a car on the trail above her house. Later that day she saw a similar car backed in at the Fay Fuller camp with people unloading it. On Sunday, she noticed the vehicle again and described it as being a "rich reddish tan but more brown than red,"[28] and later as a "bronze" color. Rose was closing up her camp between 2:00 and 3:00 that afternoon to return to her home in Bennington when she noticed a woman about thirty or forty years of age and somewhat 'hippy' walking down the trail. She was dressed in a brown leather jacket, dark beret and wore dark pants. When Rose drove down the trail fifteen minutes later, she didn't pass her on the way to the main road, some two miles away.

Mr. and Mrs. William H. Myers lived directly across from the Fay Fuller camp. They arrived at their home on Sunday, December 1st and also noticed a car backed in at the camp. About six o'clock the next morning, when Mrs. Myers let their dogs out, she noticed a tall and slender girl outside the shelter wearing a bright red jacket and dark blue pants. Later that morning, Mr. Myers noticed the car again and described it as being "rusty maroon,"[29] but didn't make note of the make and model.

Eleanora France said she had seen a similar car several times driving on the trail. Her house was about $7/10$ mile below the Fay Fuller camp. About 1:30 P.M., she noticed the car traveling up the trail and it stopped in front of her house because her dog had gone into the road and sat down. When she went to retrieve it, she saw an attractive young woman with long blonde hair, wearing red, sitting in the passenger seat. The car had an out-of-state license plate. When shown a photograph of Paula Welden, Mrs. France believed it was the same girl she had seen in the car. The timing of her observations was all wrong if the girl was Paula Welden. According to other witnesses, Paula didn't approach the Long Trail for another 2½ hours. Neither the car nor the occupants were ever found. It's likely some people who claimed they saw Paula that afternoon were mistaken in her identity. It appears there were two women in the area of the Long Trail – one presumably being Paula Welden and the other being the taller woman who was staying at the Fay Fuller camp and who was seen in the bronzy/rusty/maroon-ish automobile.

Scoutmaster Lawrence Powers and his wife, accompanied by Stephen Vince and two Boy Scouts, had gone up the Long Trail about 3:15 P.M. They parked across from Mrs. France's house and went to check on a Boy Scout camp a short distance off the trail. When they were returning to their vehicle, a car passed them going down the trail and a short time afterward a pick-up truck also went down the trail. Mr. Powers said they were going through Bennington about 4:05 P.M. When investigators later clocked the time to drive the same route Powers had taken, they determined that it took about nineteen minutes. Mr. Vince's time estimate differed slightly and he said they left the trail around 4:00 P.M.,[30] and confirmed the sighting of the car and pick-up truck descending the trail. Leonora France confirmed the movements of the Boy Scout group. Neither Mrs. France nor the members of the scout group had seen the girl on the trail, nor had they seen her talking to Ernie Whitman and his party.

Others were sure they had either seen Paula Welden or found what they believed to be evidence of her movements and came forward to help. A local taxi driver, Abe Ruskin, reported he had taken a Bennington College girl to the bus station that Sunday afternoon. When shown a photograph of Paula Welden, the cabbie couldn't positively identify her as his passenger but said it could have been her. At 2:25 P.M., a bus had departed for Pittsfield, Massachusetts thirty-five miles south, and at 3:45 P.M. another departed for Burlington, Vermont, 125 miles to the north. The Vermont Transit bus office was contacted to determine if any of the clerks or bus drivers who had driven from Bennington that Sunday remembered a girl matching Paula's description. The clerks and drivers were very busy that afternoon, it being a heavy post-Thanksgiving travel day, and couldn't recall seeing Paula specifically. After all the questioning and given the timing, State's Attorney Jerome was confident it was not Paula who rode in Mr.

Ruskin's taxi. He stated, "We have witnesses who saw her after he is reported to have picked up his fare."[31]

A couple traveling from Bennington to Brattleboro via Route 9 after midnight on the night of December 1st stopped their vehicle to put chains on their tires due to the snow.[32] They noticed fresh footprints in the snow heading away from Bennington about one mile east of Woodford Hollow. They believed they were made by a woman's flat shoe, possibly a sneaker about size 5. Thinking it was unusual for someone to be walking at that late hour in a snowstorm with no homes nearby, they followed the footprints for about 400 yards until they abruptly stopped, as if the person had gotten into an automobile. The couple also noted there was one set of car tracks in the snow on the road. The footprints were gone by the time investigators searched the area and no other clues were found.

A report that a pick-up truck had been observed going up and down the Woodford Hollow Road drew the attention of the investigators. A local man thought he had seen the truck before and assumed it belonged to someone who hunted in the area. A broadcast was made to police departments regarding a half-ton pick-up truck with New York license plates that had been seen on the Long Trail around the time Paula was seen. Within two days, Sheriff Clyde Peck had located the truck's owner. The unidentified man said he hadn't seen the Welden girl and Peck determined he had nothing to do with her disappearance, though how he came to that determination is unclear.

The temperature in the Green Mountains became progressively colder in the days following Paula's disappearance. Within two days, the temperature dropped to near zero and the local newspaper referred to "Winter's first real blast in New England."[33]

MICHAEL C. DOOLING

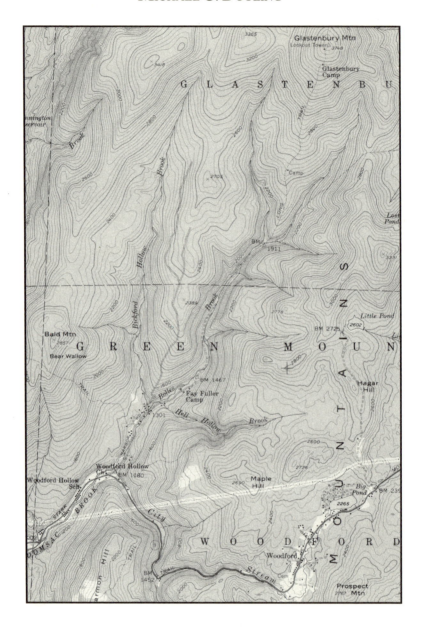

Woodford Hollow Area
Bennington Quadrangle, USGS Map, 1954

Clueless in New England

William Jerome expressed his concern, "She carried nothing such as overnight equipment to indicate she was going a long distance. She was attired in a hiking costume and wore no hat."[34] On Tuesday afternoon and continuing through Wednesday, search parties looked for Paula. The college was closed for several days to allow students and faculty to participate in the search efforts. Frank Tschorn, superintendent of grounds at the college, organized several squads of volunteers. The Bennington College student body and faculty, alongside local Boy Scouts and members of the Green Mountain Club, searched the college campus and nearby trails.

Law enforcement officials in other New England states and neighboring New York State were notified to be on the lookout for the missing student. She was described as being 5'5" tall, 123 pounds, 18 years old, pretty, blonde, blue eyes, had a scar on her left knee and a vaccination mark on her right thigh, and had a quiet disposition. She was also described as "very depressed lately and may be suffering from amnesia."[35] The multi-state alarm brought no new clues.

Interviews with college friends reinforced her mother's contention that Paula was not interested in any particular boy. Some friends said she had seemed depressed lately and a woman who worked at the college believed she had seen Paula in a college washroom on Thanksgiving night holding a letter and crying. Paula had no history of depression and Mr. Welden told the press that her letters home had always been cheerful. One theory related to the possibility that Paula wanted to start a new life:

> Girls in Paula's residence at the College stated that on Saturday night she behaved extraordinarily happy and that this was unusual for her. This evidence caused authorities to think she may have possibly decided to make a change in her life and wanted to mislead those who would attempt to trace her. They

believe she may have gone up the Long Trail as a diversion and then doubled back, possibly to make a rendezvous or to get back onto the highway where she could get a lift.[36]

Why Paula would have made such convoluted plans to hitchhike from the college to the Long Trail and then hike up the Long Trail to meet someone or to backtrack down the trail to make a rendezvous defies logic. There are far easier ways to start a new life than that, and one would think she might have brought some of her clothes and personal belongings with her.

The president of Bennington College and several others expressed the fear that Paula may have fallen on the trail and injured herself. They speculated that, as a result of such a fall, she might be suffering from amnesia and may not remember who she was or where she was from. Paula's father stated that she had no medical history of amnesia and to his knowledge had not in the past suffered a blow to the head. State's Attorney Jerome said he did not suspect Welden was the victim of foul play but "might be the victim of amnesia."[37]

A large, organized search party started at dawn on Thursday, December 5th. Sheriff Peck organized a posse and included the Bennington District State Guard Company of 120 men, nearly 300 Bennington College students and faculty, and dozens of students from Williams College in Williamstown, Massachusetts, about fourteen miles to the south. Scores of area residents and members of the local Green Mountain Club joined the effort as well. They searched the heavily-wooded Long Trail starting at Woodford Hollow. Three private airplanes from a nearby airport and two airplanes on loan to the Weldens by a family friend joined the search.

Clueless in New England

Bennington College Students Gathering to Search for Paula
Courtesy of the Bennington Banner

The nearly 500 volunteers concentrated on the area west of Glastenbury Mountain where the Blue Trail veers off toward Bald Mountain. There was some speculation that Paula may have left the Long Trail and headed toward Bickford Hollow or might have gone slightly northwest toward Bald Mountain. A member of the college faculty discovered shoe prints in the snow on the Bald Mountain Trail that might have been made by a woman's sneakers. The snow that fell on Sunday started late in the evening, which means she would have been walking in complete darkness if those were her footprints. The volunteers used a technique in which they sprinkled confetti to mark the sections they had searched. This ensured they didn't miss any areas and prevented them from being searched more than once. Seven Marine Corps planes from the Squantum, Massachusetts air station, flew over the area but were forced to stop because of low-hanging clouds. In spite of their efforts, the posse organized by the county sheriff found no trace of Paula Welden.

At the end of the day of searching, a conference was held to discuss the status of the investigation. W. Archibald Welden, State's Attorney Jerome, Bennington College president Dr. Lewis Jones, and Sheriff W. Clyde Peck attended the meeting. After the men conferred, Jerome announced that further searching of the mountain had been abandoned and the case was being turned over to the state's attorney's office for investigation. He stated that Welden had "either walked away from the college or was lured away and that a national police broadcast was being arranged."[38] The next morning, Jerome announced a $500 reward for information leading to the location of Paula Welden. The reward was offered by friends of the Welden family. Another $500 reward was offered by the townspeople of Bennington and a few days later the students at Bennington College assembled and took up a collection, raising the amount to $1,700.

A frustrated Mr. Welden visited the office of the Federal Bureau of Investigation in Albany, New York, on December 6th. Welden suspected his daughter had been abducted and sought their advice as to how to proceed. He had his doubts whether the case would be in the FBI's jurisdiction but hoped for some sort of direction from them. That night the state's attorney also contacted the FBI in Albany. The next day the head of that FBI office announced, "We will not assume jurisdiction at this time."[39] While Welden discussed his abduction theory, State's Attorney Jerome was quoted, "There isn't the slightest evidence of kidnapping or foul play in this case. In fact, there isn't any evidence of her movements after 4 P.M. Sunday."[40] In fact, there was no evidence of any of the possibilities being considered.

Mr. Welden appeared to be holding up well as he worked side by side with local authorities, college administrators and newspaper reporters. His wife was not doing so well. She remained at the family home in Stamford, confined to bed by her physician. Both of

Paula's parents were relieved Paula had not been found in the Glastenbury Mountain area. They realized if she had been located she would likely have been dead of exposure or injury. This gave them hope she might be found alive.

Sheriff Peck decided to continue searching the Long Trail area and organized another posse consisting of cadets from Norwich University in Northfield, Vermont on Friday afternoon. They were joined by faculty and students from Bennington College and by a helicopter supplied by Bell Aircraft Corporation from Niagara Falls. The helicopter landed on the campus of Bennington College and picked up *Bennington Banner* reporter Pete Stevenson. They searched the length of Route 9 that connects Bennington with Brattleboro to the east. The pilot had been instructed by the state's attorney to "look for the body of the girl alongside the highway"[41] and to search the area around Long Trail. They found nothing that afternoon, nor the next morning when they continued searching.

Missing Person Circular for Paula Welden
Courtesy of the Vermont State Police

Frustration

Paula Welden's disappearance soon gained national attention. More than two dozen reporters from New York, Boston and the Associated Press descended on the normally quiet community of Bennington. Within a few more days, more than 100 reporters and photographers were covering the story. The president of Bennington College expressed his concern that foul play was involved and that Paula's body may have been concealed. He also announced that the college would be re-opened on Friday, December 6th, having been closed since Monday in order for the faculty and student body to search for Paula.

Amidst days of disappointment and despair, alleged sightings of Paula Welden were called in from all points in the Northeast. Investigators traveled to Massachusetts, Connecticut, New York and Canada to follow up on various sightings. In Boston, someone was positive it was she who had applied for a waitressing job; a New Haven Railroad trainman claimed a passenger on a Springfield–to–New York train resembled her and he too was positive it was Paula. Another tip from customs officials at the Rouses Point, New York border crossing reported a young woman matching her description had entered Canada. The woman turned out to be a stenographer from Washington, D.C.

In Fall River, Massachusetts, someone matching Paula's description was seen with a man by a waitress at the Modern Restaurant. Ora Telletier waited on a man and woman on Monday night at 9:30. The woman matched the description of Paula Welden. The man was somewhat older, about twenty-five years of age, and showed evidence of drinking and was abusive. Telletier was convinced the girl was the missing coed, reported the sighting to the police, and related her conversation with the girl to them. She told them that when the man was paying the check, the girl waved her over to the table and asked her the distance to Bennington to which the waitress asked "Bennington where?" She clarified Bennington, Vermont, and the woman suggested she go to the bus depot to find out. The girl started saying she had to get back to Bennington over and over. She also told the waitress she had arrived in Fall River with a thousand dollars in her pocket and now had none. All the while, the girl appeared to be dazed. When the Bennington newspaper got wind of the sighting, they wired another photograph of Paula to Fall River and the woman confirmed again it was the Welden girl. The Fall River police were encouraged by the revelations of the waitress and during the night started a house to house search of rooming houses, hotels, bus depots and railroad stations. When the story was confirmed by the *Bennington Banner*, Mr. Welden was called during the night at his room in the Hotel Putnam. He spent most of that night at the newspaper office monitoring the progress of the Fall River police.

On December 6th, there was another disappearance in Bennington. Paula's father left town without disclosing his destination. It was believed he had gone to Albany to meet with the FBI, but he hadn't returned nor informed anyone of his whereabouts. Neither President Jones nor State's Attorney Jerome had heard from him. After rumors started to spread as to where he had gone, he called Dr. Jones at home and spoke to his wife. He left the message, "I don't want you to think I am lost or have disappeared. Also, I don't want the newspaper men to worry about me. I am following a hunch of my own and I may be gone for several days."[42] He did not let her know where he was or what he was doing. One rumor regarding his disappearance speculated he had been contacted by someone who knew Paula's whereabouts and he didn't want to jeopardize that avenue with publicity. Another rumor related to him finally breaking down and seeking rest away from the limelight.

One mystery was soon solved. Paula's father revealed he had

secretly gone to Fall River to further investigate the sighting by the waitress. In spite of the house-to-house search by police, it turned out to be a case of mistaken identity. After leaving Fall River, Mr. Welden went to home to Stamford and drove back to Bennington. When driving through Pittsfield, Massachusetts, he was pulled over for a traffic violation. He took the opportunity to question the state policeman about the search for his daughter. Though the trooper had heard of the case, he hadn't been given any special alert about it and told Mr. Welden that "the newsmen were carrying out the most intensive search."[43] This had been one of the problems since the beginning of the case - news reporters taking the lead in the investigation instead of a qualified law enforcement agency.

Leaving no stone unturned, Mr. Welden contacted a woman named Clara Jepson who lived a few miles south of Bennington in Pownal. Mrs. Jepson was known locally as having clairvoyant abilities and had been consulted regarding the Lindbergh baby kidnapping and the disappearance of Amelia Earhart, though without success. She helped several people locate lost items, including a diamond pin owned by John D. Rockefeller's daughter. Mrs. Jepson had also helped searchers looking for a lost hunter in 1945. She told them where to look and they found a handkerchief belonging to him, but not the hunter. Several of Paula's friends from the college had already contacted her and she directed them to search near a covered bridge, which they did, but to no avail. She told them it would be better if she could speak to a member of Paula's family. Mr. Welden was told about her supposed faculties and, although he didn't believe in that sort of thing, he consulted her. Mrs. Jepson told him that Paula had walked through a covered bridge and along a river. She also told him that his daughter was still alive and would be found in an old shack. This caused Mr. Welden to search along the banks of the Walloomsac River, over which two covered bridges crossed. He found no sign of her.

Speculation that Paula may have run off to start a new life were dispelled in a questioning session with her roommate Elizabeth Johnson. The Bennington College president spent 3½ hours talking with Johnson and became convinced that Paula was not depressed, was not distraught over anything, had simply gone for a walk, and that Paula and Elizabeth had spoken about hiking the Long Trail in the past. Elizabeth mentioned that Paula was a good hiker and could cover a lot of ground quickly. She also said that Paula was aware of the Long Trail and its many cabins and shelters along the way, though she hadn't actually hiked it.

Five days after Paula's disappearance, Dr. Jones decided to seek the aid of Vermont's State Detective Almo B. Franzoni. Almost immediately, foul play became the avenue of investigation. State's Attorney Jerome cautiously stated, "There is no direct evidence of foul play and there is no evidence that foul play took place on Glastenbury Mountain's 'Long Trail' but we are now following a theory that it might have taken place."[44]

A week after Paula disappeared the local newspaper[45] reported that three New York men had been hunting on Glastenbury Mountain the afternoon Paula disappeared. They had been seen on the Long Trail on Sunday and again early Monday morning when they checked into the Putnam Hotel at 1:20 A.M. They told the clerk they wanted to get to New York but there was no transportation at that hour. They took a room and gave their hometown as Bellmore, New York on Long Island. On Tuesday, the three men reportedly attempted to purchase train tickets to Stamford, Connecticut (the Weldens' home town) but couldn't get a direct connection. Instead, they took a train to Troy, New York, from which they could get a connection to Stamford. When they spoke to the station clerk, he informed them about Paula Welden's disappearance and he said they acted as if they hadn't known about it. Inexplicably, they told the conductor on the train they had been participating in the search for her in spite of their seeming ignorance of the events in front of the station clerk.

Another possible lead surfaced when the owner of the local Paradise Restaurant claimed a girl resembling Paula had purchased four sandwiches on Sunday morning apparently before she went to work. Paula's roommate countered this claim and said Paula had been in the room all morning. She also admitted she had been deeply studying with her back to Paula and it was possible she could have left the room and come back.

W. Archibald Welden had shown great courage under the tremendous pressure of having a daughter suddenly go missing. But signs of his immense frustration became evident at a press conference held at the home of State's Attorney William Jerome on December 9th. Almost every clue had run into a brick wall and tempers were hot. At the conference[46] Almo Franzoni made the statement, "The state authorities have done everything that is humanly possible to solve this case and if there are no new developments by tomorrow, I shall leave the case. It will then be pursued by the circularization of photographs bearing a complete description of the missing girl...I have no jurisdiction unless there is definite evidence that a crime has been committed." A normally calm Mr. Welden retorted angrily, "Just what have the state authorities done to find my daughter?" He then started criticizing Vermont's "inadequate and inefficient facilities to cope." He expressed his gratitude to the authorities who worked on the case saying they "have done everything within their power" but continued, "The difficulty is, however, that there is no organized police system within the state and for that reason much of what we would like to do must remain undone." Welden vowed to "stay on here in order to force them to keep the case open." He then pleaded to the press, "I earnestly hope that managing editors of the various newspapers covering this story will not recall their reporters. The authorities are working as hard as they can, but they are few in number. The reporters here are the sparkplugs of this investigation."

At the same press conference it was revealed that "Mr. Franzoni discovered a pair of soiled, bloodstained pink panties lying among the heavy underbrush in a deep gully about 20 feet off No. 9 highway, some 125 feet from the spot the girl left the car (*sic*) of Louis Knapp to go on toward the Long Trail."[47] For reasons unclear, police authorities held little hope they were related to Paula's disappearance. According to the same news account, the panties were shown to Mrs. Mary Garrett, Director of Admissions at Bennington. After Mrs. Garrett examined the panties, they were completely disregarded as being meaningful. It is uncertain on what basis she discounted this article of clothing and there is some confusion regarding this possible piece of evidence. According to the *Stamford Advocate*,[48] "A woman's undergarment found near the entrance to the trail was eliminated as a possible clue when the missing girl's roommate reported it did not belong to Paula." Where the garment was found (either near Knapp's house or near the Long Trail several miles away), whether or not there were two different undergarments found, and exactly who examined them is unclear.

For a brief time, police thought an important clue had emerged. The *Banner* reported[49] that a 15-year-old girl from Bennington claimed she was walking home from a church party on the evening of November 30th and two men pulled up in a car, blindfolded her and drove her to a house. There, she heard a woman with a coarse voice say, "This is not the right girl. Take her back where you found her," which they allegedly did. After the state's attorney questioned her at her home, he spoke to the press and stated, "Her story has substance." Almo Franzoni was also encouraged and said, "This might be the break in the case," spurring everyone's hopes. After more questioning, the girl confessed she was late getting home that night and created the story to keep from getting punished.

CLUELESS IN NEW ENGLAND

Another "clue" emanated from Rutland, Vermont. A man carrying a large amount of money and a revolver went into the Flory Tailor Shop to buy a suit on the morning of December 1st. He told the tailor he was going to Bennington and had a date with a blonde. The man was located and questioned, and authorities determined he was not involved with Paula's disappearance. More promising was a worrisome clue from Manchester about twenty-six miles to the north. A man and his wife had heard what they thought was a woman screaming in that vicinity on the night Paula disappeared. It was a scream unlike any they had heard before. Investigators searched the woods and marshes and concentrated on a "lovers' lane" from which the screams could have emanated. After a thorough search of the area authorities were again without a clue. Frustration was everywhere as the investigation stalled. The man in charge of the investigation, William T. Jerome, said "Every single clue and rumor has washed away."[50]

At the encouragement of author Dorothy Canfield Fisher, who lived in Arlington, Vermont, Mr. Welden contacted the governor of Vermont to seek assistance. He asked Governor Mortimer B. Proctor to contact the FBI and the Connecticut and New York state police departments on his behalf. Mr. Welden expressed the desire for scientifically trained police to join the investigation. Mrs. Fisher also sent a telegram to United States Senator George D. Aiken of Vermont to express the concerns of Vermonters and to request aid for the investigation. As a result of Welden's urging, Governor Proctor contacted Connecticut's Governor Raymond E. Baldwin for help and he agreed to provide it.

After the blow-up at the press conference, Almo Franzoni was ordered to remain on the case by Vermont's Attorney General Alban J. Parker. On the morning of December 11th, Franzoni contacted Edward J. Hickey, Connecticut's Commissioner of State Police, and asked him to send his best detective to assist the investigation. It was announced at another press conference held at the home of William Jerome that a "crack sleuth" from the Connecticut State Police would soon join the investigation. Hickey stated, "Ordinarily we do not operate in other states but Miss Welden is a Connecticut girl and we would be inclined to stretch a point, if possible."[51]

As the second press conference in two days broke up, Jerome was called to the telephone. He was heard to cry out, "Hold that man until I get there."[52] The drama was heightened all the more since he blurted out his words within earshot of reporters. Before he left, he told reporters he was on his way to Wilmington, Vermont, about twenty miles east of Bennington. He departed immediately and was accompanied by Detective Franzoni, Deputy Sheriffs James Scarey and LeRoy Dunn, and Motor Vehicle Inspectors Albert Christie and Lloyd Potter. Apparently a brownish-reddish car had been stopped by police in Wilmington. Two hours later, the six officials returned; it wasn't the right car. The drama of the moment, the over-reaction by the chief investigator, and the number of human resources used to chase a remote possibility were good examples of some of the problems that Mr. Welden had outlined in his outburst of frustration.

Realization

On December 11th, Connecticut State Police Commissioner Edward J. Hickey ordered Lieutenant Robert N. Rundle, a 35-year-old detective, and State Policewoman Dorothy Scoville to assist in the Paula Welden case. The two had worked together on several previous missing person cases and other serious criminal cases. Upon arrival in Bennington at 7:00 that evening, Rundle and Scoville met with Almo Franzoni to learn everything done to date. During the early part of the case, college officials, the local newspaper staff, and the county sheriff were primarily involved in the search and investigation. They weren't trained to document what they were doing; hence, no records were kept during the first ten days of the investigation making the task of catching up very difficult. The three met at the home of State's Attorney Jerome and were joined by Stanley Kunitz (poet/professor who assisted President Jones on the case), Motor Vehicle Inspector Albert Christie, Deputy Sheriff James Scarey, and W. Archibald Welden. Rundle and Scoville decided to conduct their own investigation and would compare findings with Vermont investigators.

William Jerome requested that news reporters not follow or interview the two visiting sleuths as they went about their work, and they agreed to hold back. He also guaranteed they would be kept apprised of every important event. Lieutenant Rundle informed the reporters that "No strings are attached to my investigating methods. I will receive full cooperation from the Vermont authorities."[53] On the 14th the *Banner* printed a letter[54] that Mr. Welden wrote to the students of Bennington College:

> To the students of Bennington:
>
> Paula's mother and I are deeply grateful to each of you. Your wholehearted participation in the

searches and the real personal concern you have expressed in so many ways have given us much needed support through trying days. Since December 3 we have been conscious of the lack of trained personnel for conducting an investigation of this nature. We have tried to bring in agencies from out of the state with no success until last evening when two investigators from the Connecticut State Police arrived here. They are now reviewing the evidence and we are hopeful that even at this late date they may uncover something which has been overlooked.

But even as the search goes forward I wanted you to know something of our feeling. Your help means so much to us.

Sincerely yours,

W. Archibald Welden

Appeals went out to hikers, campers or anyone else who was in the area near the Long Trail to contact the investigators. Rundle vowed he would "question at length anyone who was within fifty feet of Paula."[55] Working 18-hour days, Rundle and Scoville questioned anyone who might have any information. They looked into whether any member of the faculty had ever made a romantic advance toward Paula; they found no evidence of that nature. They also requested a composite photograph be created. A girl of Paula's stature was dressed as Paula had been that Sunday afternoon. They took her photograph and then superimposed a picture of Paula's face. Rundle hoped this would be a better representation of her likeness and hoped it would help people identify her.

Rundle and Scoville re-questioned all the witnesses who had seen Paula along Route 9 and on the Long Trail. The most intriguing of their interviews involved the Maxwell family who lived on the Long Trail about $^2/_{10}$ mile above Eleanor France's house. They were the last people to have seen Paula walking along the trail. Viola Maxwell and her daughter Mary reported they had seen a girl matching Paula's description heading up the trail toward the woods that afternoon. The two were coming out of their cow barn as she passed by wearing a red jacket and blue pants. She was walking north on the Long Trail at the time. When Rundle and Scoville visited the Maxwell home, they also questioned a man who was sitting in a corner of the room. The man was Alfred (Fred) Gadette (or Gaudette, depending on the source or report)[56] and was Viola Maxwell's boyfriend. He had lived with her on and off for the previous seven years. When questioned, he told the investigators he had not seen the girl resembling Paula and had been in New York State all day on December 1st.

On a second visit to the Maxwell home, Viola told police only she and Mary were home that day. Gadette was in the house at the time and was questioned again. He varied his story slightly, telling Rundle and Scoville he had left the house at 5:30 in the morning on December 1st and didn't return until about midnight. This time he said he had gone to Bennington rather than New York State. Rundle wrote in his report, "This man was very reluctant to talk to us at this time."[57]

Rundle and Scoville requested the Superintendent of Schools pull the Maxwell children out of class so they could be questioned. The school nurse accompanied the children to the town hall and each was interviewed separately. Mary Maxwell, age 15, was interviewed again and her statement differed from earlier ones. She told the investigators that, "On December 1, 1946, her mother, Stanley (her brother) and herself were the only members of the family at home...that Fred Gadette and her brother, Clarence, had gone to town early in the morning in Stratton's truck (owned by Gadette's employer William Stratton) and returned about noon. Clarence left at that time and Fred was around the house. She did not remember what time Fred left but was sure he was back for supper..."[58] She also said that Gadette used to be her mother's boyfriend but now she was seeing another man. Yet, she reported having seen her mother being hugged by Gadette. Her story was consistent with her earlier account about seeing Paula walking by their house.

Stanley Maxwell, age 12, told the investigators he was home that day until about 2:00 to 2:30 P.M., when he went with his uncle to do some chores. When he left the house, he remembered Fred Gadette being there. Preston, age 10, told them he wasn't home that day, having gone to Searsburg with his grandparents. When Clarence Maxwell, age 16, was later questioned, he told Rundle that he had ridden from his house the morning of December 1st to Bennington with Alfred Gadette. Clarence remained in Bennington and was uncertain where Gadette went afterward.

When Viola Maxwell was again questioned, she changed her story and told investigators that Gadette had returned home for lunch and then went out again, but wasn't sure where he had gone. When Sheriff Clyde Peck read her statement he told Detective Rundle that Viola had told him that Fred Gadette was home the afternoon of December 1st. Peck, Rundle and Scoville returned to Viola Maxwell's house once again for clarification. Her story changed yet again. She told them, "Fred Gadette was at the house in the morning and left in Stratton's truck. He came home for dinner (lunchtime) and left again. In the afternoon she and her daughter Mary were going to the movies and started to walk down the Long Trail. They met Fred down by the Smith house and they rode back with him. He went up the trail and turned the truck around near the old school house and then parked it by the old cow barn on the trail. Viola said he had gone into the house while she and Mary did the chores. She was sure that Alfred was in the house when the girl went by and did not know why Alfred Gadette lied when he was talking to us."[59]

Clueless in New England

With all the different versions of his whereabouts, Alfred Gadette emerged as a suspicious person in the eyes of investigators. The *Washington Post* got wind of his contradictory statements and reported that an arrest was due soon and that "a detective had discovered discrepancies in statements of a Bennington man questioned as to his whereabouts the day Miss Welden disappeared."[60] The investigators decided to bring him in for questioning and Detective Rundle, State Policewoman Scoville, Sheriff Peck, and Almo Franzoni paid him a visit at the Maxwell home. They brought him to the County Building and questioned him about his various stories. Rundle summarized his latest story in his report:

> We questioned this man for a long time as he was lying to every one of the officers all through the investigation. All during the previous interviews he denied seeing a girl on the trail. At this time he gave the following story: On November 30, 1946, he stayed at the Maxwell house. Early the next morning in company with Clarence Maxwell he went to Bennington to have William Stratton's truck repaired. He did not remember whether or not he came home for lunch. At about 3:30 P.M. he returned to the Maxwell home and before he arrived he met Viola Maxwell and Mary Maxwell walking down the trail. He picked them up and then drove to the school house and turned around. He parked the truck just above the cow barn which is just above the Maxwell house on the left of the trail. When he got to the cow barn he saw a car with Mass. registration parked in front of the Maxwell house heading down the trail. He stayed in the truck and watched while Viola and Mary went to the car and talked to the two men that were in the car. He

suspected that Viola was going out with these men and that was the reason for watching them. Viola came up to the truck with him and he was bawling her out for cheating on him. While they were in the truck he saw the girl that was wearing a red jacket go up the trail. After the men left he went into the house and again started arguing with Viola. When Viola's mother and father returned Viola went upstairs to bed and he left the house in a rage and went across the street to the shack where he spent the rest of the night.[61]

In follow-up questioning with Viola Maxwell that same day, she again lied about Fred Gadette's whereabouts and when confronted with Fred's story admitted she had made up the earlier stories. She said she knew the two men in the other vehicle, said they lived in North Adams, and told the investigators she had been out with them before. Yet, she didn't know their names – only referring to them as "Benj." and "Doc." After the questioning was completed, both Viola and Fred were released. Detective Franzoni wrote in one of his reports, "The reason (for lying) given by both Gaudette and Mrs. Maxwell was that she is applying for a divorce and did not want it known she was courting Gaudette as it might affect her getting it."[62] It seems likely that suspicions might have arisen due to the fact he had been a boarder in the house on and off for seven years. The investigators succeeded in tracking down Benjamin Bruno and William ("Doc") Mathews, both of North Adams, Massachusetts, and verified the most recent story told to them by Gadette. They added that they too had seen the girl in the red coat walk by.

CLUELESS IN NEW ENGLAND

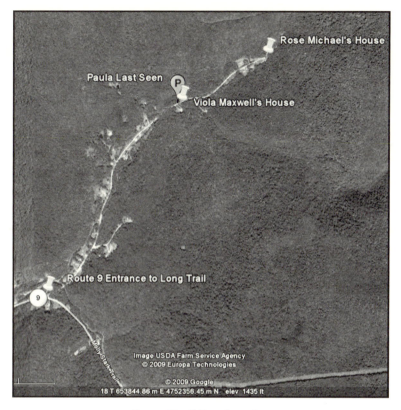

Long Trail Landmarks
Google Earth

In another twist to this story, a Mrs. W. Champaign of South Hero, Vermont told authorities that she had a dream about the case. In her dream, Paula was walking on the Long Trail and came to a black car. "She asked the man for a ride and he said he would give her a ride but he was going to have a cup of tea first. He asked her in and while there he attacked her, choking her to death and then took up the linoleum and the floor of this camp, there placing her underneath the floor, and the linoleum was put back and a stove over this spot."[63] The camp she described was the third camp on the right side of the trail. It was unclear if she was referring to the third camp on the way up the trail or the one on the way down. If her frame of reference was descending from the top of the trail, the third structure on the right was the shack where Fred Gadette primarily stayed. Detective Franzoni searched the area but found nothing.

Rundle and Scoville drove and walked the route Paula appeared to have taken. They calculated the distances from Paula's residence, Dewey House, at Bennington College and made notations of various landmarks, points where sightings occurred, etc. They determined that if Paula did not receive another ride after Louis Knapp dropped her off at his house she would have had to walk a total of 5.4 miles (including 3.6 miles after he dropped her off).[64]

Approx. Time	Landmark	Miles
	Dewey House	0.0
	College gate	1.1
3:00 P.M.	Louis Knapp picked up girl	1.8
	Intersection 67A and U.S. 7	2.3
3:15 P.M.	Louis Knapp's house	5.9
3:30 P.M.	Cora Mallory's house	7.7
3:40 P.M.	Foot of Long Trail at Route 9	8.3
4:00 P.M.	Ernie Whitman encounter	
	Mrs. France's house	9.3
(Paula last seen)	Mrs. Maxwell's house	9.5
	Mr. & Mrs. Myers house	10.0
	Fay Fuller shelter	10.0
	Rose Michael's house	10.2

After more than two weeks passed since Paula's disappearance, Mr. Welden decided there was nothing more he could do in Bennington. He said he would not return "unless something important comes up."[65] With a promise that the state's attorney would call him daily with an update, he made the difficult decision to leave. With the newly-dedicated carillon bells from the Methodist Church ringing in the distance on Sunday morning, he packed up his daughter's belongings in her dormitory room. He placed them in the back of his Buick coupe and drove off the campus onto Route 67A where Paula had hitchhiked a ride from Louis Knapp, and drove through Bennington center.

It's not known if he drove Route 9 east through Woodford Hollow one more time. There were two logical routes home. One headed south on Route 7 into Massachusetts, east of the Taconic Range that shields New York State's Lebanon Valley. It then crossed the Connecticut border, skirted around the little town of Salisbury and continued south toward Stamford. The alternative route was to drive west for a short distance into New York State and head south on Route 22, along the borders of Massachusetts and Connecticut. That route eventually connected to Connecticut's Merritt Parkway to reach Stamford. Mr. Welden left Bennington after expending every ounce of his energy in the search for his daughter. He believed in his heart she had been taken against her will, hoped she was still alive, but realized she probably was not.

The next big effort in the Welden disappearance occurred two days after Mr. Welden left. Investigators focused their attention on a gravel bank near the south gate of Bennington College, near the knoll where Paula was seen by Danny Fager. Jesse Watson, Chief Fish and Game Warden, had noticed there had been a landslide there around the time of Paula's disappearance. When Watson inspected the gravel bank he found a hemlock twig at the crest of the 75-foot mound. Having heard of Paula's interest in botany he thought perhaps she had climbed the embankment to reach nearby hemlock trees to take a cutting, perhaps triggered a landslide and became caught up in it. He brought it to the attention of authorities early in the investigation but they dismissed it.

Excavating the Gravel Pit
Courtesy of the Bennington Banner

After no progress was made in the case, the possibility of a landslide was re-considered. State's Attorney Jerome said it might be possible to discount the statements from people who claimed to have seen Paula. The authorities decided to excavate the entire pile of dirt in spite of many witnesses who had seen, spoken to, or given a ride to Paula. They borrowed a steam shovel and a bulldozer from a local contractor and worked into the night of December 17th under three floodlights loaned by the Bennington Fire Department. William Dailey, who owned the equipment, stated his men wouldn't stop until all the dirt from the landslide had been moved. Harry Mattison, who himself had been buried up to his chest the previous year in a landslide at the same pit, and Ray Welch worked the steam shovels throughout the night. A crowd of curious and interested onlookers watched and endured temperatures dipping down to zero.

Clueless in New England

Twelve hours later, the workmen had removed more that 500 tons of gravel and as with all the other leads in this case, found nothing.

Mr. Welden and his attorney, Charles R. Covert of Stamford, returned to Bennington for a day to discuss the terms of two rewards. A $5,000 reward was offered to anyone who found Paula alive and a $2,000 reward to anyone who found her dead. At this time, the *Bennington Evening Banner* published a letter[66] from Paula's father:

> To the People of Bennington:
>
> Your many courtesies, your sympathy, and the great help extended to me in the search for my daughter, Paula, are appreciated more than I can say.
>
> Mrs. Welden and I are deeply grateful to you. We still have hope but whatever may develop, we will always remember your heartfelt interest and goodwill in voluntarily doing all in your power to help.
>
> Sincerely yours,
> W. Archibald Welden

It must have seemed an eternity since Paula's disappearance the weekend after Thanksgiving. The weeks leading up to Christmas were anything but joyous for the Welden family. The usual seasonal cheer was replaced by overwhelming sadness and the inevitable feeling that Paula was gone from their lives forever. Two days before Christmas, a desperate Mr. Welden made an impassioned plea on a Stamford radio station for Paula to come home. His plea was printed in several newspapers[67] as well:

Paula:

If this broadcast reaches you - know that we love you. Whatever may have prompted you to leave us, if you have gone off of your own free will, be sure we will find a better answer to your problem by working it out together. Just pick up the nearest telephone and ask for me. You won't need change. The operator will reverse the charges. I'll come for you immediately, wherever you are, and bring you back home to your mother and sisters who love you so much and miss you so terribly. Lots of love from us all.

Signed,
Daddy

As the winter days became colder so did the search for Paula. Mass searches ended and searching by Bennington College students ground to a halt in the new year. As part of the college's curriculum, students were required to spend the first two months of the year gaining practical experience in their fields of study. Many went back to their home-towns to gain these experiences, others went to distant cities. The college campus became a virtual ghost town, haunted by the inexplicable disappearance of one of its own.

Deciding to conduct its own investigation into the disappearance of their hometown girl, the *Stamford Advocate* hired a private detective agency to investigate Paula's disappearance. In January 1947, Fred Deisler and Shelby Williams, of the famed Raymond C. Schindler Detective Agency in New York City, quietly investigated the case for three weeks. One area of their investigation involved the direction Paula may have gone on the Long Trail, if she had gotten there at all. According to the Schindler Agency investigation, the sign indicating the Long Trail heading north toward Glastenbury Mountain was not up the day Paula was looking for it. However, the sign for the continuation of the trail toward Sucker Pond to the south was present. The private investigators believed it was possible, in spite of eyewitnesses who saw Paula on the Long Trail to the north, that she could have taken the south trail. Searchers had spent a great deal of effort exploring the northern route and relatively little on the southern route. They also considered the possibility that Paula hiked the Long Trail north and tried to circle back to the college campus through the woods rather than retrace her steps back to Route 9, and got lost.

The Schindler Agency detectives investigated what happened to Paula shortly after Louis Knapp said he dropped her off. When Knapp arrived home, he told his wife and daughter how he had given a ride to a hitchhiker and let her out in front of their house. A few minutes after he entered the house, his daughter went outside to call her own daughter to dinner. She didn't notice anyone on the road. From Knapp's house, there was an unobstructed view down the road toward the Long Trail for about a half-mile. If Paula had been walking down the road, she should have been visible to Knapp's daughter. It is possible another driver picked her up as soon as she was dropped off and she would have been driven out of sight in a short time. Knapp's house was about 2½ miles from the Long Trail entrance and it is highly likely Paula continued to hitchhike the remaining distance, though no drivers came forward saying they had picked her up. It's also possible Knapp's daughter simply didn't notice her. The Schindler Agency investigators concluded, "there is but slight hope the Bennington College sophomore still lives and great probability that she is dead of foul play."[68]

Pursuing the foul play theory, Shelby Williams suggested having Louis Knapp tested with a lie detector. The *Stamford Advocate* editor said the newspaper would pick up the tab. State investigators decided to test other witnesses or suspects in the case as well. In April 1947, eight people in some way associated with the case or who had seen Paula on the day she disappeared were evaluated in Williamstown, Massachusetts, at the Williamstown Inn. Leonarde Keeler conducted the lie-detector testing. Keeler was one of the founders and chief proponent of the field of polygraphy. He had studied under John Larson, considered the inventor of the polygraph.

The eight subjects tested were Louis Knapp (who gave Paula a ride toward the Long Trail), Fred Gadette and Viola Maxwell (who had both lied to investigators and had seen Paula while arguing), Benjamin Bruno (one of the two men sitting in a car whom Fred thought Viola was dating), Elizabeth Johnson (Paula's roommate and the source of considerable information about the days leading up to her disappearance), Harold Colvin (who took Paula to the square dance Thanksgiving night), Allan Schauffler (who had hiked and camped with Paula and whom Mrs. Welden sensed she particularly liked),[69] and a man named Carl Mattison. This last name appears only once in the files provided by the Vermont State Police. Other than the fact that he worked at Bennington College, his relationship to the investigation is unknown. According to Franzoni's report, "On Tuesday night, April 29, 1947, we completed our test and all were found not to have lied."[70] A few newspapers mistakenly reported one of the eight subjects fled afterwards. This was a false report that was corrected by Vermont's Attorney General Clifton Parker.

Polygraph testing was relatively primitive (first developed in the 1920s) and the field was still in its early stages in the 1940s. Although widely used since then by police departments, its validity and reliability was (and still is today) questioned by the scientific community. Validity refers to whether the lie detector is testing what it is designed to test – detecting lies. Reliability refers to the consistency from one test to the next or from one examiner to another. In those early days of polygraphs techniques for questioning, the length of the test, and even how much to inflate the blood pressure cuff had not been standardized. So suspect is the polygraph as a valid and reliable tool it still is not allowed in the courtroom as evidence. In the 1940s, it was estimated that lie detector testing had an error rate of about forty percent. In spite of that, the technique was becoming widely used by police organizations as a tool of the trade.

Part of a lie detector's mystique isn't so much in the physiological reactions to questioning but relates to the drama surrounding its use: the imposing set-up; whether the subject is convinced of its power; how he reacts when "caught" in a lie; and the follow-up interrogation that ensues. Innocents have been determined to be liars and guilty parties have passed with flying colors. Subjects can react badly to questions because of nerves or fear of being determined a liar when they are telling the truth; other subjects learn to fool the machine by training themselves not to react or by self-inducing reactions when the questions are of a general, non-threatening nature thereby throwing off the baseline readings. Some subjects who exhibit certain personality syndromes, such as Antisocial Personality Disorder, have little or no sense of guilt or respect for the law. Some of them are incapable of reacting, even at the physiological level, to questions about their guilt or innocence. They simply are not fazed.

There appears to have been some conflict between the investigating authorities in Vermont and the *Stamford Advocate*/Schindler Detective Agency alliance. After the lie detector results were printed in the Stamford newspaper and in Associated Press articles, the Bennington College president said he had no knowledge of such a thing and concluded it must have been done "as a private enterprise" and continued, "there are a lot of amateur sleuths in the woods investigating this case."[71] The state's attorney and Sheriff John J. Maloney, who had replaced W. Clyde Peck, denied any knowledge of such a test having taken place.

As spring approached, small groups of people searched for Paula, mostly on Glastenbury Mountain. Plans were made for a more elaborate search once the winter weather broke and the snow melted. In April the new governor of Vermont, Ernest W. Gibson, announced the search and hinted he had "highly confidential"[72] information regarding the case. A few weeks later, Gibson stated, that Paula may have been "lost, shot by hunters or a victim of amnesia...from the weight of the evidence there is absolutely no motive for suicide."[73] Strangely, he didn't mention the possibility of abduction or murder, an angle the Connecticut detectives and Almo Franzoni had been busy investigating.

During the weeks, months and years after Paula disappeared, Bennington investigators continued to chase clues: a maroon car that resembled the one they were looking for, but wasn't; a young man who had attempted to choke a girl in Bennington; a car thief from Connecticut who had been in Bennington the day before Paula disappeared; and other sightings including a girl resembling Paula in a taxi cab in Quebec. They even investigated if there was a connection between the Welden case and the Black Dahlia murder case in Los Angeles in January 1947. Franzoni told a reporter, "In my 25 years of police experience, this is the most baffling case I've ever been connected with...We've tracked down every indication of foul play and we've run up against a blank wall on every lead."[74] Nothing could be connected to Paula Welden.

On May 24, 1947, after the heavy winter snows had melted, a large search party combed the Long Trail area for two days, looking for clues or for Paula's remains. The search was coordinated by Sheriff Maloney, and more than 100 volunteers searched twenty-four square miles of the mountains. Sixty men from the Vermont National Guard participated in the search and nearly twenty newspapermen from the Northeast covered the story. Both of Paula's parents and two of her sisters went to Bennington. Mrs.

Welden watched from afar while her husband and daughters actively participated. After seeing the search area on Glastenbury Mountain through binoculars for the first time, Mrs. Welden told reporters, "Hope can never die no matter how low you get. But I may have to face the fact that I may never see Paula again." Later that day she commented, "It certainly looks hopeless, doesn't it?"[75]

On that day, Mrs. Welden also expressed her concern regarding the possibility of foul play. "I still think there is a possibility of foul play, although there is no evidence in that direction. It seems hard to believe that Paula would do anything foolish. She was completely naïve. She was most innocent. Paula's character would never permit her to believe that anyone would do her harm. And for that reason she would readily have taken a hitchhike ride with anyone who might have come along. The only possibility would be because of Paula's innocence."[76]

Paula's Parents & Sisters Examining Map with Almo Franzoni (C)
Courtesy of the Bennington Banner

Two discoveries held promise for a short while. A discarded pair of torn, greasy jeans was found but they weren't Paula's size or style according to her roommate. Searchers noticed an odor resembling a decaying animal or human near Bickford Hollow, but they couldn't locate the source. At the end of the second day, Mr. Welden commented he was "...satisfied by the planned search and it was quite conclusive that Paula had not been lost. There is still a possibility in my mind that a crime could have been committed and that her body lies in this area. All evidence points to the fact that she headed toward Long Trail, between Glastenbury and Bald mountains. Foul play could have been possible in Bennington or any other place. I would welcome any evidence that she is not dead."[77]

The new State's Attorney, James Holden, appeared entrenched in the position that there was no evidence of foul play. Though true, there wasn't any evidence of anything else either. A few days later, he backed off his position and admitted foul play was one of many theories being investigated. On June 23, 1947, a conference of various agencies and individuals was held to discuss the case but no new news was presented. Mr. Welden attended the meeting and once again was critical of Vermont's handling of the case:

> The conference proved again that the investigation in connection with the disappearance of Paula Welden was handicapped by the lack of adequate and experienced handling from the outset. It is quite clear now that some of the most logical and vital elements were given no more than a cursory glance. These matters, if investigated promptly after December 1, might have answered the question that the people of the nation are asking today. What has become of Paula Welden? It is bewildering to one in my position to realize that, in this modern day, the state of Vermont is probably no more advanced in the facility for handling an investigation of this kind than it must have been 100 years ago.[78]

Clueless in New England

As time closed in on the first anniversary of Paula's disappearance, leads continued to be investigated. In September 1947, police received a report that a man had behaved strangely when he saw a group of men approach an old mine shaft off Route 113 about 2½ hours drive northeast of Bennington. A group of men, some of whom were from Stamford, Connecticut, had been trying to find a horse show in the area and on their return decided to stop at an old copper mine – the Ely mine – north of West Fairlee in an area known as "Copperfield." The mine was located about ¾ mile off the main road. When they pulled off the road to park, a passing pick-up truck with Vermont plates stopped and pulled in near them. A man got out of the truck and walked very quickly over to the group. He asked what they were doing and they told him they were going to the old copper mine. They asked him if he had ever been there and he replied he hadn't. The man then said he wanted to join their group to look at the mine and as they walked toward it he started talking as if he knew the area very well and later claimed he had once been there to remove some machinery. He walked over to one of the shafts and said it smelled, yet no one else noticed any odor.

The man seemed anxious the entire time and the group consensus was he seemed to be afraid they would find something he wanted to remain hidden. He left when they did and they reported his strange behavior to the police. The police could not make any connection with Paula Welden's disappearance though Mr. Welden later speculated someone may have disposed of his daughter's body in the mineshaft. State troopers searched the area near the mine and entered one tunnel about 1500 feet. They discovered the shafts were filled with water and the support structures were weak making it dangerous to go any farther. The areas they did search revealed nothing suspicious and they concluded "it would be unreasonable to assume that the Welden girl is in any section of the mine."[79]

In a strange coincidence in late December 1947, police in

Charleston, South Carolina reported a girl resembling Paula Welden had been brought in for questioning. A tourist camp operator thought she looked like a picture of Paula she had seen. The girl identified herself as Mary Louise Garrett. She fit the published description of Welden almost perfectly – height, complexion, scars, teeth irregularities and dental fillings. One critical difference was difficult to explain away – Paula had blue eyes but the girl in Charleston had brown. Garrett claimed she had no connection whatsoever with the missing girl. The police put her in touch with Mrs. Welden over the telephone and after their conversation Mrs. Welden was convinced she was not her daughter. Police determined she was Mary Garrett of Neelville, Missouri. The thing that is most unusual about this girl is that her name "Mary Garrett" was the same name as the Director of Admissions at Bennington College who first called the authorities to report Paula missing. Nothing more than sheer coincidence.

As the years passed, fewer and fewer sightings, suspects or clues of any sort surfaced. In 1948, Vermont authorities questioned an armed robber arrested in Cambridge, Massachusetts who had an article about Paula in his pocket and a sketch resembling her in his room. He had once visited the Glastenbury area of Vermont but denied any direct knowledge of her disappearance. In 1950, a Western Union Telegraph Company messenger from New York City read a follow-up article about the Paula Welden case and reported that he had delivered a package to a woman at the Empire State Building who signed that name. The subsequent investigation shed no further light on the sighting. A man from Suffield, Connecticut was arrested for intoxication and told police he had married Paula Welden. He was interrogated by Connecticut State Police and was subsequently charged with giving false information to police. An anonymous caller to the Vermont State Police in 1950 told them Paula was murdered by three men and her body discarded in the sewage system underneath Bennington College. Although the police suspected the call smelled of a hoax the septic tanks were completely emptied and examined for her remains and none were found.

In 1952, based on a tip from a "mystery" witness, law enforcement authorities investigated a report that Paula's body had been buried under a porch or in a cellar near the Long Trail. One newspaper reported, "The tip came from relatives of the girl friend of the suspect, a 35-year-old lumberjack. The relatives said that on her death bed the girl quoted the lumberjack as saying he knew where Paula Welden was buried."[80] Other reports mentioned that Alfred Gadette had told his friend and local fern picker Ike Smith that he knew within 100 feet where Paula was buried.[81]

Gadette, who at this time lived in Readsboro, Vermont, a few miles southeast of Bennington, was again questioned by police for nine hours and he told them he had seen a girl in a red jacket and blue jeans walking up the Long Trail that Sunday afternoon. He told police he had been joking about knowing where she was buried as a way to increase local prestige. This, of course, was not the first time Gadette was questioned by police and his answers in 1952 matched, for the most part, what he had told them in his earlier lie detector test. According to news accounts, "He admitted that after seeing Paula walk up the trail, he went into his home and argued with his girl friend. Then he said he stormed from the house, and wheeled his truck up the trail in the direction Paula had walked...the direction was opposite to the road leading to Bennington."[82] This was <u>significantly</u> different from a Connecticut State Police interview in 1946. Detective Rundle then wrote that Gadette said he "left the house in a rage and went across the street to the shack where he spent the rest of the night."[83] When asked why he drove up the trail, he said, "for a ride and a pastime."[84]

At the time of the re-questioning of Gadette, State's Attorney John B. Harte was away for National Guard training at Camp

Devens and Reuben Levin was appointed acting state's attorney for twenty-eight days. Levin, believing they finally had a good clue, told reporters the case was close to a solution. Five minutes before his short term as state's attorney was up, Levin performed his last official act. He issued a search warrant to look for the remains of Paula Welden in the cellar or on the grounds of the two suspect bungalows, one named "Shangri-La," in Bickford Hollow. Reuben told reporters, "Even if the man in question confessed to our satisfaction, we couldn't arrest him unless we could find the girl's body. We couldn't even hold him for more than 24 hours unless we could produce the corpus delicti."[85]

When State's Attorney Harte returned the next day, he determined there wasn't enough evidence to pursue that line of inquiry. He believed Gadette had just been joking and halted the excavation work before it started. As in the rest of the investigation, the solution to the case continued to be elusive.

In 1953, a dump-picker found bones in a homemade wooden box in a Pownal, Vermont dump about twelve miles from where Paula Welden disappeared. A Bennington plumber searching for old oil drums uncovered the small box that appeared to contain a complete, albeit disarranged, human skeleton. The size of the skeleton indicated a person who was slightly built and suspicions immediately arose that it could be Paula's remains. Though the bones appeared several years old, the box had only recently been placed in the dump. State pathologist Joseph W. Spellman conjectured the bones had been used by medical students for study and had been discarded improperly. A man from North Adams, Massachusetts who had once lived in Pownal contacted Sheriff Maloney and confessed he had discarded the box. He had found the box and its contents in the barn next to his Pownal home. The home had previously been owned by the late Dr. J. L. Niles and the bones were believed to be his specimens. Niles' granddaughter confirmed he used the skeleton in his practice and this line of inquiry was brought to a close.

Two years after Paula disappeared, Mr. Welden wrote his scenario of events tying together several clues in a lengthy letter to the Commissioner of Public Safety Merritt A. Edson. Welden spent more time than anyone trying to piece together what had happened to his daughter. He did not believe she had become lost or committed suicide; he believed she had met with foul play. A portion of his theory follows:[86]

> As far as is known or surmised, Paula walked up the section of Long Trail starting from route 9 at about 4:00 P.M. Fifty minutes to an hour of brisk walking would have brought her to a footbridge crossing Glastonbury (*sic*) Stream...Paula would have arrived at this point about 4:50 or 5:00 P.M., twenty minutes to half an hour after darkness had set in. Darkness would have set in not later than 4:30 P.M. on December 1, as the sky was over cast with several inches of snow which fell later that evening. The temperature was dropping rapidly. With the silence accenting the roar of the stream through the boulder strewn bed some ten or twelve feet below the question is "Did Paula cross the stream?" I think it is not probable. Two nights later accompanied by two men, each of us with flashlights, I had to think twice before crossing.
>
> ...Paula proceeded on the Long Trail past the intersection at Bickford Hollow Trail, at which point she was last seen. Between there and the footbridge darkness would fall and Paula probably turned and retraced her path to route 9. She would arrive there between 5:00 and 5:30 P.M. From here to the college gate takes about 14 minutes by car. Though she may have started to walk, she would fully realize the lateness of the hour and probably tried to get a lift. Assuming this occurred before 6:00 P.M., the driver,

talking with her passing through Bennington, may have decided to take advantage of the situation and instead of turning off on route 67A, continued on route 7 toward Manchester. On the evening of December 1st, a householder on the outskirts of Manchester reported hearing a scream. Both he and his wife heard the scream and described it as being distinctly human, but such as they had never heard before…About five hundred feet beyond the house the Chief of Police indicated a space used frequently by couples parking. A scream could have been heard at the house from this point…

We may never know if Paula was assaulted or abducted on her way up the trail, or on her way back down, or whether she made it all the way down to Route 9 where a driver took advantage of an attractive female hitchhiker. It is equally unlikely that we will ever know whether she was murdered and buried somewhere in the vicinity of the Long Trail, or driven points north to Manchester and beyond, or perhaps driven west to New York State and her body dumped off some mountain road in the Taconic Range far away from the search parties and investigators.

Paula's story continues to be resurrected on the anniversaries of her disappearance. Articles in the *Bennington Banner* and other newspapers appeared yearly at first and less frequently as the years passed. On the 10th anniversary, the *Banner* wrote, "There are few who still believe that she is alive. But there are more who think she is dead and that the case has never been near a solution. It remains one of the major mysteries of this era…it looks now as though the mystery of what actually happened will never be known. However, strange things happen and the files are never closed."[87] On the 12th anniversary, Almo Franzoni was interviewed and said, "I don't think we ever had a good clue."[88]

Clueless in New England

Paula literally vanished that Sunday afternoon. So disconcerting was the fact that someone could completely evaporate that other disappearances in the area began to take on new meaning. Soon the entire series of them developed into one of Vermont's most enduring legends.

Chapter II

"One becomes melancholy as he thinks of the number of men, women and children who have started on the one-way path which, like parallel lines, runs to infinity."

Hartford Courant, 5 June 1927

CLUELESS IN NEW ENGLAND

The Green Mountains

Paula Welden wasn't the first person whose disappearance in the Green Mountains caused a stir. Over the years, many people have become lost in the thousands of square miles of wilderness in Vermont. One famous disappearance in particular bears a haunting coincidence with the Paula Welden case. Though not discussed much today, it was the most famous disappearance in Vermont's history up to the time Paula Welden vanished.

The town was Manchester, about a 25-mile drive north of Bennington using modern means of transportation. But the year was 1812. A man with the first name of Russell had married Sally Boorn and they had several children. Russell was somewhat mentally unbalanced, had difficulty keeping a job and couldn't support his family. By 1812, his wife and children had gone to live with her parents, resulting in bitter feelings toward him by the family. He also had a penchant for roaming around Manchester and sometimes wandered away from town for long periods of time. Several times during his marriage he disappeared for extended durations, sometimes for as long as eight to ten months, but he had always returned home.

On May 10, 1812, Russell disappeared again and no one thought much about it. After several years passed, however, rumors that he had been murdered began to circulate. The local gossip was that his two brothers-in-law, Stephen and Jesse Boorn, had been seen fighting with him shortly before he disappeared. One of the brothers had intimated to someone he knew that Russell was dead. Their uncle, Amos Boorn, claimed that Russell had come to him in three dreams and told him he had been murdered. In the dream, Russell beseeched Amos to follow him to the spot where he had been buried.

When Amos actually went to the location he had dreamed about, a four-foot square hole under the site where a house had once stood, he found a large knife, a penknife and a button. Russell's wife identified the large knife and button as belonging to her husband. Nearby, he discovered bones in the roots of a tree stump. Physicians believed them to be human bones and assumed they were all that was left of poor, hapless Russell.

Seven years after Russell disappeared, an investigation ensued and Jesse Boorn was arrested and questioned at length. After several days of confinement and "every art made use of to induce him to criminate himself and his brother, and, being told that a confession would probably be the means of obtaining his liberty,"[89] he confessed, sort of. Actually, he pointed the finger at his brother Stephen. He told his inquisitors that Stephen had told him he had hit Russell and "…laid him where no one could find him."[90]

Stephen was arrested and imprisoned, separated from his bother Jesse. In late August of 1819, Stephen wrote a confession stating he had committed the crime. The two brothers were tried in the Manchester court. Besides the confession, the court heard from Russell's son, Lewis, who had seen Russell and the brothers engaged in the quarrel and had seen Stephen strike Russell over the head with a tree limb. A jailhouse confession, a witness to a quarrel and considerable circumstantial evidence led the jury to find the two men guilty in one hour. Jesse was sentenced to life imprisonment but Stephen was destined to hang.

Then, everything changed. The Boorns' defense attorney decided to place advertisements in various newspapers asking if anyone had seen the missing Russell. His supposed rationale was that if Russell had simply gone for a very long walk he might be living in the Northeast and someone might know him. Perhaps the victim wasn't a victim and was still alive. After a month passed, and five weeks before Stephen was scheduled to hang, a Methodist preacher in Shrewsbury, New Jersey, wrote a letter to a newspaper indicating that Russell might be found living there. He described Russell and mentioned some names of people whom Russell was related to and familiar with in Manchester. A Mr. Whelply, who had once lived in Manchester, went to New Jersey and brought back the man people believed to be Russell.

The two returned to Manchester by stagecoach, stopping in Bennington where a crowd of curious people quickly formed. A few of Russell's acquaintances were in the crowd and he reportedly recognized them and called them by their names. Word was sent ahead to Manchester that Russell was near. By the time the stage arrived, crowds had gathered to see this modern-day Lazarus. Russell seemed to be familiar with individuals and events that had happened in the town. Stephen Boorn was brought forth in chains to confront his "victim." When he saw his chains, Russell asked, "What is that for?" "Because they say I murdered you," Stephen replied. In a dramatic moment, Russell told him, "You never hurt me."[91] When Russell saw his wife, he simply stated, "That's all over with,"[92] and pretty much ignored her. He also didn't seem to know his own children when they were brought forward. But that didn't matter; he was befuddled and confused and not quite right, after all.

Two men convicted of murder, yet the victim was still alive? Within a short time, the court released the Boorn brothers from prison. A week after he arrived, Russell left Manchester and never returned. This true story has been the subject of much debate over the years. Some believe Russell had simply gone away, the brothers confessed under duress, and the real man actually returned to Manchester. Others believe the man who claimed to be Russell and had come back to town was an imposter. They believe that Russell had in fact been murdered, and the courts and the public had been outwitted by a very clever charade carried out by people who wanted the Boorns released. There is good evidence to support this belief.

Forty years after Russell "returned" to Manchester, Jesse Boorn became involved with a band of counterfeiters. He told a man who wanted to join the gang that he and his brother had murdered their brother-in-law and got away with it. He went on to tell him that the man claiming to be Russell was an imposter. The man who claimed he wanted to join the gang was actually an imposter himself. He was a deputy U.S. Marshal working undercover.

One other intriguing piece of evidence lends credence to the imposter theory. When the minister from New Jersey who "found" Russell wrote to the newspaper and mentioned names of people who Russell knew in Manchester, he mentioned the name "Chase" who was a judge. Judge Dudley Chase presided over the Boorn brothers' trial but would not have been known to Russell. He was a Vermont Supreme Court Justice and didn't reside in Manchester.

Interestingly, a young man surfaced in the Paula Welden case, more than a century later, who had the same name as the 19th century Russell. The man who disappeared 134 years earlier was named Russell Colvin, the name of one of the "kitchen boys" from Bennington College. Russell and his brother Harold were friends with Paula and had attended square dances together. A few days before Paula disappeared, the 20th century Russell Colvin had arranged for his brother Harold and Paula to go on a date to the Thanksgiving night square dance. Paula disappeared three days later and, unfortunately, never returned.

Closer to the time when Paula Welden vanished were the disappearances of several men, women and children of various ages from 1945 to 1950. There is a core group of five individuals associated with these occurrences, including Paula Welden. Over time, this cluster of missing people became known as the "Long Trail Disappearances," named for the trail that runs the length of Vermont where Paula was last seen. The area has been referred to as "The Bennington Triangle" and the imagined perpetrator of unknown horrors as "The Bennington Monster" and "The Mad Murderer of the Long Trail." In fact, only three of the disappearances occurred near the Long Trail and not all were in Bennington County. But the nicknames persist and have become entrenched in the lore of southern Vermont. Superstition and fear of the unknown have led to speculations about everything from a crazed killer to alien abductions in order to explain the series of mysterious vanishings. No discussion of Paula Welden's disappearance should exclude the backcloth against which it is generally compared.

A seasoned hunter who was last seen on Glastenbury Mountain was the first person to disappear in the Long Trail cluster. Middie Rivers, age 74 and from Bennington, disappeared near Bickford Hollow on Glastenbury Mountain the year before Paula Welden thumbed a ride to Woodford Hollow. On Friday, November 9, 1945, Rivers went hunting with a group of men including his son-in-law, Joseph Lauzon, Jr. On Monday, Rivers and Lauzon left their camp at 7:30 A.M., hiked to a fork in the trail and there the two men trod off in different directions. Rivers indicated he would be back for lunch but hadn't returned to camp by 3:00 that afternoon. He wasn't familiar with the Bickford Hollow area and had been warned against going over the ridge between the Bickford and Glastenbury streams. Around 4:00 in the afternoon on Monday, Hollis Armstrong saw Rivers over the ridge between Glastenbury Mountain and Bald Mountain to the west. When he was questioned by Armstrong, Rivers said he had no fear of getting lost and headed away from the direction of the camp. When he didn't return, the rest of the hunting party went looking for him but found no sign of him.

Members of his hunting party notified the fire department and on Tuesday a search of the Bickford Hollow area was undertaken. About twenty men, organized by Fire Chief Wallace Mattison, searched but found no sign of the missing hunter. Middie's friends feared he might have become ill or injured and was unable to move. Fortunately, because the weather was unusually mild, Rivers had a reasonable chance of surviving out in the wilderness. On Wednesday morning at 6:00 A.M., the fire department sounded the emergency call of 3-3-3 for volunteers to help in the search. About twenty local men (mostly firefighters) were joined by fifteen of Rivers' co-workers from the BenMont Paper Company. The small search party scoured the area for the better part of the day but found nothing. On Thursday, Chief Mattison put out a request for volunteers through the local newspaper, hoping to recruit 500 men to assist in the search on Friday. Everyone was to meet at the Bradford Hook fire station at seven in the morning. Only forty showed up. The local newspaper[93] reported:

> Somewhere in the deep woods up Bickford Hollow, Middie Rivers, 74-year-old lover of hunting and fishing, is lying dead or alive. If alive, he's pinning his faith on the hope that his home town will stand by him and send out enough men to find him. Middie didn't know it – but this morning that hope was blasted when no more than 40 men responded to Fire Chief Mattison's appeal for 500 men.

The poor turnout was in part blamed on the number of residents who themselves were off hunting in the mountains around Bennington and staying at numerous camps. Most of them weren't even aware that Rivers was missing. A systematic search was conducted using the available human resources, including high school students, Boy Scouts and members of the Civil Air Patrol. Hope was dimming for finding Rivers alive as he had been missing for four days and nights with nighttime temperatures starting to drop below freezing. Some hope was revived when the Harbour family from Woodford Hollow reported they had heard two gunshots every morning around 6:00 A.M. for several days. Some believed it could have been Middie Rivers attempting to signal searchers but trying to conserve his ammunition.

In an effort to recruit more men, the Bennington selectmen offered a stipend of $4.00 per day to anyone willing to participate in the search effort. The publicity effort helped bring out more volunteers but very few accepted the money. Soldiers from Fort Devens, Massachsuetts were asked to join in the search. Ninety soldiers arrived in Bennington and were housed at the State Armory. On Sunday morning, six days after Middie Rivers disappeared, they entered the woods and searched it thoroughly, walking twenty feet apart to cover as much territory as possible. They found no clues. The newspaper reported, "No trace whatever was found, not a footprint, not a campfire, or an overnight shelter."[94]

Mrs. Jepson, the clairvoyant from Pownal who would later be involved in the Paula Welden case, was contacted by Middie's friends and asked for help in finding him. She told them where to look for their hunting companion. When they searched the area, they found a handkerchief with money tied in one corner that belonged to the missing hunter...but no sign of Middie Rivers himself.

Authorities contacted Middie's only son and gave him the bad news. He was in the Navy Reserve and had just returned to the United States after serving in the Pacific. On Tuesday morning, the search for Middie Rivers was abandoned. Snow had begun to cover the ground. Even so, another search took place a week later organized by Joseph Lauzon and included the local Boy Scouts and some of the hunters who had been on the mountain all week. The original theories about the reason for Middie's disappearance related to having gotten lost, ill, injured, or perhaps he had fallen into a river and was swept downstream. The prevailing theory at the end of the search was the same one believed to have happened to Bennington hunter John Harbour in 1897, also near Bickford Hollow. It was believed Middie Rivers had been accidentally shot and killed by another hunter, who then hid the body so he wouldn't be found out.

The third in the series of disappearances happened three years to the day after Paula Welden walked into history when a World War I veteran vanished during a bus ride to Bennington. On December 1st, 1949, 68-year-old James E. Tedford boarded a bus in St. Albans, Vermont, on his way to the Soldiers' Home in Bennington. He had been visiting relatives in the northern Vermont town of Franklin and family members put him on a Vermont Transit bus to return home. Tedford, who was wearing a gray suit and his army overcoat, never arrived at the Soldiers' Home. No one is sure when he disappeared but he was reportedly seen on the bus at the stop before Bennington. No one noticed him get off and he was never found.

Tedford was described by sources at the Soldiers' Home as "physically well but mentally ill."[95] They also said that Tedford had told them that once he left he wouldn't return. Law enforcement officials checked all the stops between St. Albans and Bennington and no one could remember him getting off at any of them. A state policeman in Brattleboro (about forty miles east of Bennington) remembered seeing a man fitting Tedford's description getting off a bus there, but he couldn't locate him. A twelve-state alarm was issued to other police departments but James Tedford was never seen again.

Another year, another disappearance; this time, an eight-year-old child. On October 12, 1950 a boy named Paul Criston Jepson, nicknamed "Buddy," vanished without a trace. The Jepson family lived on a farm on White Creek Road in Shaftsbury a few miles north of Bennington. Paul's father was the local tax collector and he and his wife were caretakers for the Bennington town dump. They also raised livestock and kept sixty-five pigs at the dump. According to a newspaper account, Paul had never gone to school because of "nervous defects."[96] Paul's mother had gone to the dump to move the pigs from one section to another and left Paul sitting on the front seat of her truck. When she returned, Paul was gone. Sometime between 3:00 and 4:00 P.M. Paul had either left the truck on his own or was taken by someone.

Mrs. Jepson looked for her son and then went to a nearby home, where she called her husband. He contacted Sheriff Maloney who called the State Fish and Game Warden. A small posse was organized and searched the five-acre dump for Paul. The local newspaper described the scene that night in the vicinity of the dump, "It was a dreary night for the volunteers. There were scattering warm showers during the early evening and about 10 o'clock these changed to a cold heavy rain and later to a drizzle. The searchers became thoroughly chilled. They were "chilled" in other ways too as flood lights were played on the dump on the huge pigs or hogs. The noise of the grunting pigs and the smell of the dump gave none too pleasant atmosphere. Occasional large rats running around the area added to its gruesomeness."[97]

Not finding Paul, the sheriff called the fire department and the state police for assistance and the combined force searched about fifty acres of woods. At about midnight, "Little Queenie," a bloodhound, was brought in from Keene, New Hampshire and followed Paul's scent to the intersection of East Road and Chapel Road, where it was lost. It was likely the rain that night had destroyed the scent. The bloodhound stopped searching about 2:30 in the morning. Mr. Jepson, who had told police that Paul had walked off in the past and had shown a "yen" to go into the mountains, maintained a watch all night in his truck near this intersection.

A public alarm was sounded the next day and a new search was undertaken with a hundred community volunteers including selectmen, Boy Scouts and employees at a local manufacturing plant. A few footprints that might have been Paul's were found on the side of a road, and a dog was heard barking around 4:30 the previous afternoon, lending some encouragement to the searchers. They searched the woods and roadsides in the shadow of Glastenbury Mountain but found nothing.

The next day the sub-headline on the front page of the *Bennington Banner* read, "8-Year-Old Boy Becomes Third to Disappear in this Area in Past Five Years." The newspaper made the observation, "The mystery of Paul's disappearance and not a single clue to work on, makes the third such case of a missing person in practically the same area during the past five years."[98] This reference alluded to Middie Rivers, Paula Welden and Paul Jepson. No one knew where James Tedford actually disappeared, whereas the other three were in the general vicinity of Glastenbury Mountain when last seen. Two people disappearing under unexplained circumstances and now three. People started to wonder.

The United States Coast Guard sent planes from Boston and a helicopter from Salem to join the search. The search party grew with volunteers from more manufacturing facilities, firemen, and individuals from other communities in Vermont and nearby New York State. A dozen searchers revisited the dump looking for possible cave-ins, probing suspect areas with potato hooks and poles. Throughout the weekend more than 250 volunteers continued to search the woodland and swamps for Paul. The local PTA and the Red Cross set up feeding stations for the searchers. An area covering six square miles was carefully gone over on foot but no clue as to Paul's whereabouts was found. On Sunday night Sheriff Maloney called off the search. His men needed a rest and he believed if Paul had been lost in the woods he had likely died of exposure or starvation.

Suspicions were raised that foul play may have been a factor. Six sexual psychopaths had recently escaped from a New Hampshire mental hospital. Five of the six had been caught and one was thought to be hiding out in New York State. Officials examined the possibility that the escapee or someone else had taken Paul, or that he had been hit by a car and dumped somewhere else by the driver to avoid detection. Mr. Jepson told authorities that Paul was careless around automobiles. Some believed the reason the bloodhound lost Paul's trail may not have been due to the rain but due to a catastrophic event that happened at that intersection – that Paul had been hit by a car at that location.

As in the Paula Welden and Middie Rivers cases, in which psychic Clara Jepson (no relation to the Shaftesbury Jepsons) was consulted, Paul's grandmother and family friends also consulted a psychic. Mrs. Aura Horton, of Rupert, Vermont predicted Paul would be found dead on Sunday and the man who snatched him would be caught. She also told them the man buried Paul at the foot of the mountains in a pile of leaves with brush covering it. Unfortunately (or perhaps fortunately), no such discovery was made.

State Detective Almo Frazoni, veteran of the Paula Welden case, was brought in to assist the investigation. He re-interviewed anyone who had information about the disappearance but was unable to uncover anything else. Rumors were starting to run through the community implicating the parents in Paul's disappearance. The police questioned them extensively and Mr. Jepson hired a lawyer. Mr. Jepson decided any questioning of his family would only be done in the presence of their attorney. The police contended it was routine questioning, but with no clues whatsoever to the contrary the police started to focus on some sort of foul play as a possibility.

The disappearance, search, investigation and curiosity seekers were taking their toll on the Jepsons. Caring for their farm, twenty-nine head of cattle and the dozens of pigs at the dump became difficult as they searched for their son and kept up with the investigation. So many telephone inquiries were being made to the Jepson family they started refusing all out-of-town calls.

Several reports came in that people had seen the boy; one said he was seen near a quarry area. Nothing was found to indicate the boy had been there. Another organized search was conducted near the dump in the vicinity of East and Chapel Roads on the following Sunday. About twenty-five volunteers, including three Vermont state troopers, joined Paul Jepson's father to search an area near Bald Mountain. A search helicopter from Westover Field flew over the area. Jesse Watson, the State Fish and Game Warden who discovered the gravel pit landslide in the Paula Welden disappearance, accompanied the pilot as a scout. The searchers were unsuccessful in finding any trace of Paul and Monday's headlines read, "Sunday's Clueless Search for Jepson Boy Ends Use of Volunteers."

After Sunday, authorities felt they had searched the area sufficiently and were going to pursue other leads. Twenty-one children from the Chapel School, near the intersection where the bloodhound lost the scent, were interviewed by police with their teacher. The schoolchildren were dismissed at 3:00 and 3:30 P.M. (depending on their grade level) on the day Paul went missing. Their dismissal coincided with the approximate time Paul disappeared. None of the students remembered seeing him, nor any strange people or vehicles. Members of a hooked rug class held at that time in a nearby home were questioned and they saw nothing.

With no trace of Paul Jepson, and little hope of him being alive, interest in the case began to wane. Two days after the final organized search for Paul, the association of James Tedford was made in the series of disappearances with the *Bennington Banner* headline reading, "Missing Jepson Youngster Makes Fourth Disappearance of Local Persons in 5 years."[99] The strange string of events was noticed by others as well. An article about the disappearances in the Albany (N.Y.) *Times Union* was quoted locally, "Vermont's killer of mankind, concealer of murder, and mocker of authority today is the chief suspect in the recent disappearance of Paul "Buddy" Jepson. The Green Mountains, peaceful and beautiful from afar, yet treacherous and merciless when intruded upon are believed to have swallowed another victim – a child who loved the rugged hills."[100] It wouldn't be long before another disappearance drew the rapt attention of more volunteers and the public at large, and became the fifth in the series of strange events in the Bennington area.

Just sixteen days after Paul Jepson disappeared from the front seat of his mother's truck, a 53-year-old woman hunting in the woods with her cousin went missing. Freida Langer, her husband Max and her cousin Herbert Elsner (all from North Adams, Massachusetts) owned a camp about 150 feet from the edge of Somerset Reservoir on the eastern side of Glastenbury Mountain. They built their camp in the town of Somerset in 1936 and had visited it nearly every weekend since. The camp was located nine miles from the main road and was accessible only via a gravel road. Somerset was considered an unorganized town consisting of 18,000 acres of wilderness and had a population of just two in 1950.

About 1:00 P.M. on Saturday, October 28, 1950, the Langers and Herbert Elsner arrived at the camp. Around 3:00 P.M., Elsner decided to leave camp to hunt partridge but Max's rheumatism in his left leg was bothering him and he stayed behind. Freida decided to accompany Elsner and hiked into the woods with him. According to Herb Elsner's account of the events following their departure, forty-five minutes into the hike Freida slipped and fell into a shallow brook and became drenched. At this point, she and Elsner were about a half mile from camp. Elsner escorted her most of the way back so she could change into dry clothes. He helped her climb a bank almost overlooking their camp 150 yards away. She decided to walk the rest of the way by herself. Elsner continued hunting until dusk and then returned to camp. He then learned from Max that

Freida hadn't returned.

After searching the area around the camp, Max Langer reported his wife missing to Lawrence "Bucky" Leonard, the caretaker for the nearby Somerset Reservoir and dam, and one of Somerset's two residents. He contacted the Vermont State Police in Brattleboro and Corporal Foster Corliss organized a night search of the area. Vermont state troopers were brought in from around the state to assist in the search. The state police and other volunteers went right to work searching the woods around the camp. The local newspaper reported, "Officials were so busy searching Saturday night and Sunday that they had little opportunity to question Mr. Langer and Mr. Elsner in too much detail. These two and other persons will be interviewed more closely today to get any possible further information."[101] It seems since Elsner was the only person with Freida during her last minutes before disappearing and was the source of the story about her falling into the brook and her movements thereafter, it would have been critically important to interview him in great detail. Such was not the case.

Since there were no visible footprints in the dirt near the reservoir, the authorities involved decided it wasn't a very high probability she could have fallen in. Instead, they spent their efforts looking elsewhere. The small search party found no sign of her. On Sunday, a bloodhound was brought in by Sheriff Arthur Jennison but when it picked up a scent in the woods it kept backtracking to the camp. Rains the night before may have hampered the dog's ability to follow the scent further.

Freida's husband told police that she had a brain tumor removed eighteen months earlier and had been in good health ever since. Prior to her surgery she suffered from fainting spells but they had subsided since her operation. They all feared that in the course of falling into the brook she may have struck her head, became disoriented and lost her way. She might have inadvertently walked away from the camp into dense woods. Other than that explanation, it was difficult to explain how she could have gotten so lost, so close to her camp, in territory she knew so well, during the last hour of daylight.

Searching continued on Monday and Tuesday with helicopters traversing all the wooded areas and swamps near the reservoir at low altitude. The crews felt that if Mrs. Langer was in the "hard woods," they would have seen her. Side by side with the state police were game wardens, members of hunting clubs, and volunteers from surrounding towns. Time was running out as temperatures were dropping every night. Boats were placed in the reservoir manned by Westover Field's Army Air-Rescue group from Chicopee. Coast Guard helicopters from Salem, Massachusetts and New London, Connecticut were brought into service at various times to search the heavily wooded areas and the reservoir from the air. Max Langer offered a $100 reward to whomever found Freida, but neither the searchers on land, in the air, nor those on water had any luck.

On Wednesday, thirteen handpicked state policemen were assigned to the case with a directive from General Merritt Edson, State Director of Public Safety, to stay on the job until Freida Langer was found dead or alive or until there was a satisfactory explanation for her disappearance. Pressure was mounting for the authorities to do something. This was now the fifth unsolved disappearance in the area and everyone was well aware of that fact. A few days later, the Windham County State's Attorney Edward A. John was quoted, "We have got to crack this one. The public is demanding it."[102] Some hopes were raised when footprints were found in a swampy area six miles east of Somerset Reservoir. Searchers also found freshly broken twigs and branches they interpreted as evidence that Freida was in a dazed condition and trying to attract attention. Although no actual sighting of the woman was made, and there was no certainty that the footprints belonged to Freida, the authorities in charge of the search were encouraged. Sheriff Patrick O'Keefe of Brattleboro prematurely and naively told reporters, "We hope to have her out of the woods alive by mid-afternoon."[103]

As the searching continued with no clues, the police focused on the possibility of foul play. A closed inquest was to be held at the Municipal Courtroom in Brattleboro at 2:30 P.M. on November 3rd. Max Langer and Herbert Elsner were expected to participate, but on the morning of the inquest Elsner disappeared. He arose early and left the Langer camp before 7:00 A.M., telling Langer he was getting an early start searching for Freida. Large headlines in the local newspaper that evening read, "ELSNER, COUSIN OF MRS. LANGER, MISSING."[104] No one heard or saw Elsner throughout the morning, and authorities started looking for him. They found his car at mid-day parked near the trail leading to a camp owned by Pearl Gates. His camp was located on the stream known as East Branch that runs south from the reservoir for a few miles where it joins the Deerfield River. The Deerfield River intersects Route 9 about twelve miles east of the Woodford Hollow Long Trail entrance.

That morning, three search teams converged on the area where the footprints had been found. Instead of joining the organized search parties, Elsner reportedly teamed up with four employees of Greylock Mills of North Adams, where Max Langer worked as a textile loom repairman. They started walking the five or six miles toward the swamp where the footprints were found. Somehow Elsner, an experienced woodsman, became separated from the rest of his party. At 2:30 P.M., he was found returning alone from the Flood Dam by state police Sergeant Foster Corliss. He was immediately driven to Brattleboro for the inquest that had started at two o'clock. There is no indication in published sources why Elsner decided to search the woods only a few hours before the inquest. He may have thought he would return in time to make it to Brattleboro. Elsner would have had to leave the Langer camp by at least 1:00 P.M. to make it to his appointment. Or perhaps he had gotten lost after he was separated from the rest of his party and was later than anticipated. His behavior was thought to be puzzling, given the timing and importance of the Brattleboro inquiry.

The inquest was held at the office of Judge Ernest F. Perry and State's Attorney Edward John conducted much of the questioning. He reportedly grilled Langer and Elsner about the circumstances surrounding Freida's disappearance but learned nothing new. Max Langer voluntarily took a lie detector test on portable polygraph equipment borrowed from the Connecticut State Police. Elsner was exhausted from his trek into the woods earlier that day and the polygraph examiner determined he was too tired to be a good subject. Voluntary lie detector tests were conducted with both men in Providence a few days later. That equipment was considered more powerful and the test was administered by an expert who knew the effect of high blood pressure on test results, a condition that Max Langer suffered. After four hours of testing each man, both passed.

The state's attorney was interested in pursuing several "puzzling aspects" of the case that "just don't add up."[105] It didn't make sense that Freida simply disappeared, especially being so close to her camp as reported by Elsner. She was experienced in the woods and it wasn't like her to get lost, especially in such familiar territory. Had she had a seizure as a result of her former medical condition searchers felt she would have been found quickly and close by. Police started interviewing her friends and relatives in North Adams and Williamstown, Mass., to learn about Freida's background, and that of her husband and cousin, looking for anything that might shed light on her disappearance including the possibility of foul play. According to North Adams neighbors, "...the Langers and Elsner have been for years a closely knit unit with few close friends."[106] They didn't believe it was possible that either Freida's husband or Elsner could have done deliberate harm to her.

Back on the mountain, it was determined the footprints in the swampy area may not have been as fresh as originally thought but small groups of searchers continued to look in the area. Bucky Leonard, the reservoir's caretaker, continued to believe the footprints were Freida's. He believed the size of the imprint indicated a woman's boot and no other woman would likely be hiking in such a remote, dense area. The footprints could be followed for a mile but there was no sign of Freida. Small search parties continued looking throughout the week of November 6th.

One more large-scale effort under the leadership of General Edson was made to find Mrs. Langer. With orders to "Get out and find that body,"[107] police and local volunteers were joined by five companies of National Guard troops from North Adams and Pittsfield, Massachusetts. A new consideration was on the table. Authorities speculated that Freida could accidentally have been shot by a hunter and her body hidden, the same theory considered in the Middie Rivers case. On Saturday morning, more than 300 volunteers descended on the area near Somerset Dam, the Salvation Army set up their portable soup kitchens, and the search began. For two days, the area was searched by the largest mass search in the history of Vermont. Forty-five gallons of soup, 100 gallons of coffee, 175 dozen donuts, 1,250 sandwiches and 18,000 acres of wood and swamp were devoured that weekend…but the searchers were starved for even one clue.

After this substantial effort, the search was abandoned as was all hope of finding Freida Langer dead or alive. The hunting season for deer was to start in three days and large numbers of extra people in the woods would only endanger more lives. Deer hunters were alerted to keep an eye out for Freida's body, but not to disturb it if they found it. Max Langer and Herbert Elsner both returned to North Adams after the search and were understandably despondent. Elsner vowed he would never return to the camp in Somerset.

CLUELESS IN NEW ENGLAND

No amount of searching would reveal Freida Langer's whereabouts. It took the spring thaw and rushing waters to release her body from a watery grave. Just after noon on May 12, 1951, James Renton and Herman Lincoln of Stamford, Vermont, were fishing in the East Branch of the Deerfield River and stumbled upon Freida's body immersed in a foot of water among the tall weeds and grass. The site where they found her was near the Flood Dam in Somerset about three miles downstream from the reservoir and about 3½ miles from where she was last seen alive near her camp. The two fishermen had parked their car at Bucky Leonard's place, at the southern end of the Somerset Reservoir, and it took them three hours to hike back to inform him of their discovery.

According to news accounts, "Mrs. Langer's body was found lying on its back, in somewhat of a gruesome condition. One hand was gone and most of the head in but skeleton form. The heavy hunting clothing, however, helped keep the remainder of the body fairly intact. Her coat was buttoned up to her chin."[108] Her body might have been found earlier had search parties looked along the East Branch. Most of their efforts concentrated on the woods and the reservoir. Authorities had believed the water in the stream wasn't deep enough to drown a person. They believed this in spite of the fact that Pearl Gates had hiked to that area a few days after Freida disappeared and "could not cross the East Branch as it was too high at that time."[109]

It wasn't until 7:00 in the evening that authorities managed to get into the area where Freida's body had been found. By the time they finished their examination of the body and a search of the surrounding area, it was nearly dark. With considerable difficulty caused by a badly waterlogged and heavy body, narrow paths only illuminated by flashlights, dense undergrowth, and an unstable and narrow suspension bridge they had to cross, they carried Freida out of the woods. State's Attorney Edward John, state policemen and

Dr. Milton Wolf, who cursorily examined the remains, concluded Freida died of "accidental drowning." Freida's identity was confirmed by the metal plate on her skull, surgically placed there when she had her brain tumor removed. The investigators surmised she must have become disoriented and fatigued and "in an exhausted condition fell down a slight embankment into a deep water hole"[110] in the East Branch. She could have walked that distance in two to three hours from the point where Elsner supposedly left her near the cabin. Or, she could have ended up in the East Branch much nearer the cabin and was swept downstream.

After the recovery party returned at 11:15 P.M., authorities went to the Langer camp to deliver the news. Langer and Elsner were there for the weekend to conduct their own search. The *Banner* reported, "Upon arrival at the Langer camp, Mr. Langer received the message with muffled emotion but later burst out into tears. Mr. Elsner, more stoic, could not help but release a few tears."[111] Vermont's Attorney General, Clifton A. Parker, called for a stay in the burial of Freida's remains so further investigation could be conducted. State's Attorney Edward John spoke to him on the telephone and convinced him that all indications were it was a simple drowning case and the stay was lifted. An autopsy would have been performed only if there were suspicious circumstances surrounding the case or foul play was suspected. Because nothing of that sort was believed to be the case, no autopsy was conducted.

Their conclusion meant that Freida Langer had fallen into streams twice that day, the second time being fatal. Herb Elsner was the last person to see her alive, claimed he was with her when she fell into a stream the first time, and behaved oddly just prior to the inquest in Brattleboro. That morning Elsner had gone looking for Freida in the Flood Dam area, parked his car at a cabin near the East Branch, and became separated from the small search party that had joined him. Perhaps something unfortunate did happen along the river the day Freida disappeared and he thought that if he could find her body he would prevent possible embarrassment at the inquest. The collection of circumstances certainly doesn't make him a killer, intentional or accidental, but it did raise some suspicions about him. Unfortunately, whether he knew more than he admitted may never be known.

It seems unlikely the five disappearances on and near Glastenbury Mountain were related to one another. Examining the similarities and differences among the Rivers, Welden, Tedford, Jepson and Langer cases, one is hard-pressed to find many similarities other than geography and time period: a 74-year-old hunter who hiked into unfamiliar territory against advice from another hunter; an attractive college student who was seen on the Long Trail and who may have attempted to hitchhike back to campus; an elderly man with diminished mental capacity who apparently stepped off a bus early because he didn't want to return to the Soldiers' Home; a young boy with an undefined mental handicap who had in the past wandered away from his parents; and a woman who ostensibly had fallen into a stream, became disoriented, later fell into another stream and drowned. It seems the details of all these cases will remain secrets closely guarded by the Green Mountains.

Chapter III

"...twice is coincidence,"

Ian Fleming, *Goldfinger*

Connie Smith
Courtesy of Nels J. Smith

Belgo Road

Lakeville is one of several villages comprising the town of Salisbury, Connecticut. It rests in the northwestern part of the state, nestled in the corner created by Massachusetts and New York. True to its name, Lakeville sports six lakes and several ponds within its borders. Two lakes are located near the town center and are named Lake Wononscopomuc and Lake Wononpakook (both pronounced just as they look). The Housatonic River intersects Salisbury on its journey south to Long Island Sound and the Appalachian Trail meanders through the outskirts of town. The hills in Connecticut's northwest corner are the foothills of the Berkshire Mountains to the north, referred to simply as "The Berkshires."

Iron mining was the important industry here during the 18th and 19th centuries. The Ethan Allen Forge in Lakeville cast iron cannons for use by the Continental Army during the American Revolution, and the guns of the USS *Constellation* are said to have been forged there in the mid-19th century. Ethan Allen, who founded the forge, lived in this community until he headed to Vermont to lead the Green Mountain Boys. The largest of the quarry pits on Ore Hill was closed in 1923. It is filled with water and is a deep, man-made pond about a mile from the New York state line.

With all its lakes, streams, horse farms, rolling hills and steep slopes, Salisbury has been a popular vacation area in summer and winter. Besides the relaxing activities of fishing, boating and swimming, Salisbury was famous for several competitive sporting events. Fox hunting was an annual winter event for many years dating back to 1929 and attracted participants from all over the Northeast. The Lebanon Valley Hunt Club used the revered White Hart Inn as its local headquarters and some thirty of its members would spend an afternoon chasing a red fox until "it had been run to earth at the conclusion of a four-mile chase."[112] The Annual Lakeville Horse Show, started in 1937, was held in July and attracted horses of all categories, their owners, and competitive riders. In the dead of winter, Salisbury becomes a destination for skiers and is most famous for its ski jump competitions. The first annual winter carnival held at Salisbury's Satre Hill, with a drop of 250 feet in a span of only 624 feet, was held in 1927 and continues to this day.

Yet, in spite of the annual influx of vacationers and sportsmen, the town of fewer than 4,000 residents has managed to maintain its character, charm and prestige over the years. It is also home to two esteemed, college preparatory schools – The Hotchkiss School and Salisbury School. One couldn't find a more pleasant spot to live or visit...a beautiful setting accented by rivers, lakes and ponds...farmland and horse farms...quaint architecture and elegant summer homes. Sparsely settled, peaceful, secluded and relatively untouched by many of the negative influences of the outside world; that is pretty much how Salisbury is today and how it was in the 1950s.

Even crime has been a relatively unusual event in Salisbury. There was the time the post office was robbed in 1929. Three men from New York broke into the building through a rear window and blew the safe with explosives. Besides cash, they stole stamps, parcel post packages, private stock certificates, money order blanks, and five sacks of first class mail. Federal agents caught up with the out-of-town culprits two years later.

The old-timers might have remembered the elderly chiropractor who murdered his wife back in 1924. Dr. Joseph Spoth had a practice in the village of Lakeville and was in the midst of divorce proceedings when he and his wife had an argument. A lead pipe was near-at-hand and he hammered her head with it twice; she died two days later. The newspaper reported, "It is alleged that Spoth and his wife were not on friendly terms and that the assault took place when she called him a name which he resented."[113] He was convicted and spent ten years in prison. As shocking as it was, his crime didn't tarnish the image of Lakeville; after all, the actual murder took place at his home in the nearby town of Sharon.

In 1940, poaching captured the attention of authorities when fishermen were found dipping their lines in Lake Wononscopomuc before the legal fishing season began. The State Board of Fisheries & Game and the Connecticut State Police initiated a campaign to prevent these violations and errant anglers would pay stiff fines for their transgressions. But poaching of a different sort resulted in the arrest of one of Lakeville's residents a few years later. An unemployed man in his early twenties was arrested with a bond set at $1,000 for the malicious killing of cattle. One October day in 1949, he went into a neighbor's pasture, gun in hand, and killed a cow. From the unfortunate animal's hindquarters, he proceeded to "cut off the best steaks to take home."[114] He left the rest of the cow's carcass in the pasture and also left behind enough clues at the crime scene, including a long trail of blood, to result in his capture.

One crime the town of Salisbury would like to forget goes back to its very foundation. According to the earliest printed historical account[115] of the town's formation, the name "Salisbury" was derived from one of the early settlers – a Mr. William Salisbury who lived near the center of town and later moved to New York State. Reverend Joseph Crossman, a minister in Salisbury from 1796 to 1812, wrote an historical discourse about the town in 1803 in which he noted, "It is currently reported, and by good authority, that this Mr. Salisbury, after moving from here, had an unruly servant girl who had run away from him; that he went after her, bound her with a rope, and tied her to his horse, then rode so as to pull her down, and drawed her in such a cruel manner that she died in consequence of the abuse." According to Rev. Crossman's account, Mr. Salisbury was convicted of murder and sentenced to be hanged. Due to the influence of friends, his sentence was delayed until he turned 100 years of age. He apparently was never hanged.

William Salisbury's great-granddaughter took offense to the story and in 1879 wrote to a magazine that had re-published it.[116] Rachel Salisbury clarified that the servant girl had not been tied to the horse but that William Salisbury himself held the other end of the leash while he was riding his steed. Her version has the servant girl deciding to go no further, stopping and tugging on the rope. This action spooked the horse and caused him to sprint, dragging the girl and the rider as well. She claimed William Salisbury was acquitted; it was the servant girl's fault.

Over the years, the origin of the town's name was either forgotten, ignored, or conveniently re-written. When Malcolm Rudd wrote a history of the town[117] in 1899, he never mentioned the origin of the town's name, even though his work went to great lengths to provide the origins of the native Algonquin names that referred to the area and the lakes within Salisbury's boundaries.

Perhaps in an attempt to re-invent the town's history, when Salisbury's Scoville Library was built in 1895 a bas-relief that reportedly had once hung in the Salisbury Cathedral in England was mounted above the fireplace. The local minister, Rev. John Calvin Goddard, had personally made the request to the Salisbury Cathedral. In 1938, a Federal Writers Project guide to Connecticut mentioned that the town's name was taken from the city of Salisbury in England. There is something dignified about having a town named after a medieval, cathedral city in Wiltshire, England. Certainly, no one would want their town named after a man who tied up his servant, leashed her and dragged her on a rock-strewn road to her death. But re-writing history doesn't change history; it just sweeps the remains of some poor servant girl under the rug, hoping no one will notice.

Clueless in New England

Removed from the parochial concerns of local historians and the crimes of so long ago is Camp Sloane, a YMCA summer camp on the west shore of Lake Wononpakook. Located off Indian Mountain Road in the western part of Salisbury in the village of Lakeville, it has some 270 acres and is surrounded by lakes, hills, woods, fields and farmland. Across the road from the camp entrance is a large gentleman's cattle farm formerly owned by Samuel Berke, CEO of Mr. Boston Distillers. Berke raised prize-winning Guernsey cattle and, in 1952, his bull Green Meads Count was selected Grand Champion by the Connecticut Guernsey Cattle Club. Down the road from the camp is the prestigious Indian Mountain School, a boarding school for elementary age students. In the 1950s, Camp Sloane and its pastoral setting provided a true out-in-the-country experience for children and teens.

Camp Sloane was opened in 1928 by the Westchester County, New York YMCA and mainly served children from the Westchester vicinity. The camp was a typical summer camp with swimming, horseback riding, crafts, nature programs, athletics and hiking. Campers who became accomplished in these areas were recognized with a Camp Sloane patch with each area of specialty delineated. The patch included the camp motto - "Others" - indicating the importance of others over self, a working principle of the camp. When a camper reached a certain level of competence in a given area, a glass gemstone would be glued to the patch. The youngsters lived in tents containing eight campers and they were expected to keep their tents neat and clean; passing tent inspection would earn them another gem on the camper's patch. An outdoor chapel – The Chapel in the Birches – was located on the grounds and religious services were held there on Sundays. The campers' waking moments were filled with scheduled activities and also included cookouts with campers from neighboring tents, campfires and singing, talent shows, and even watching the occasional movie.

MICHAEL C. DOOLING

Camper's Patch from Camp Sloane in the 1950s
Author's Collection

In 1952, ten-year-old Constance Christine Smith was a first-time camper at Camp Sloane. She was the daughter of Mrs. Helen Jensen Smith and Peter Smith of Sundance, Wyoming. Mr. Smith was a prosperous rancher and an imposing man, standing 6'7" tall. Divorced, the Smiths lived on neighboring ranches and Connie lived with her mother. Her father had remarried and Connie was at his ranch frequently. Connie's grandfather was former Wyoming Governor Nels H. Smith, who served from 1939 to 1943.

This was Connie's first time at a summer camp and she was planning to stay at Camp Sloane for a month. Located in a tranquil setting, Camp Sloane seemed to be the perfect place to send a child to gain new experiences, build confidence, and develop teamwork and leadership skills. Well, perhaps practically perfect. The camp had its share of problems over the years. In 1940, New York camper George Winterich of Ossining, developed appendicitis and septicemia while at camp. He was sent to Sharon Hospital where he had his appendix removed but he died July 14th from the blood poisoning that ravaged his body. The boy's father, respected journalist and editor John T. Winterich, filed a civil lawsuit claiming negligence against Camp Sloane. The lawsuit was unsuccessful and a jury dismissed the case in 1944.

That same summer there was an outbreak of food poisoning at the camp affecting sixty campers. When the Connecticut State Police and State Board of Health investigated the Winterich boy's death and the food poisoning incidents, they discovered the camp physician, Dr. S. Oscar Fry of New York, didn't have a license to practice medicine in Connecticut. In the course of the investigation, Dr. Eugene Lamoureaux of the State Board of Health visited the camp and discovered that "…case records signed by Dr. Fry and the equipment in the camp's four-room infirmary indicated that Dr. Fry was practicing medicine." This was in direct contradiction to what Camp Sloane's Director Ernest P. Roberts had told him, that "…the New York physician had been engaged merely to render first aid and maintain a general check on the health of the campers."[118] Dr. Fry was arrested for failing to obtain a Connecticut practicing certificate and Ernest Roberts was arrested for aiding and abetting him. The two pleaded *nolo contendere* and Litchfield Superior Court Judge P. B. O'Sullivan imposed a $100 fine on each. This was not an insignificant fine in 1940. Based on the Consumer Price Index, it would be more than $1,500 in today's dollars.

Two seasons after the Winterich boy died and food poisoning ravaged the camp, another tragedy hit.[119] An 18-year-old dishwasher at Camp Sloane, Clarence Brown of Richmond, Virginia, arrived on June 17, 1942 to work for the summer. Two days later, he and a companion were paddling a canoe on Lake Wononpakook. The canoe capsized and Clarence drowned. A boy onshore witnessed the accident, jumped into the water and swam toward the two, managing to save the other boy. Connecticut state policemen were called in and recovered his body. For the ten years before Connie Smith first walked into her tent, Camp Sloane had been relatively problem-free. Ernest "Gov." Roberts, who had been in charge of the camp since 1938 (and who had lied to investigators about the role of the camp physician), was still Camp Director.

Camp Sloane's Waterfront
Undated Postcard

Connie was always an outdoors person, loved horses and horseback riding, was accustomed to camping and enjoyed being in the woods. According to her mother, who visited her nearly two weeks into her stay, she was enjoying her time at Camp Sloane. Connie had turned ten on July 11th and her mom went to see her in Lakeville. "She was very enthused about camp the last time I saw her on July 13th, and very excited about a square dance the girls were to have with the boys of the camp on the following Friday, and about the horse show[120] she was to be in on Saturday. She asked if she could stay longer than planned, but I explained to her that we would be leaving for Wyoming shortly after her month at camp was up, so it was impossible."[121] In spite of Connie's enthusiasm about the camp, all may not have been as idyllic as Mrs. Smith believed.

According to camp staff, during the evening of July 15th, Connie received a minor injury in a fall down the steps from her platform tent. The injury wasn't considered serious and she was given an ice pack for her sore hip. On the morning of July 16th, "Connie stated that she felt better and was involved in a little horseplay with the other girls in the tent which resulted in Connie getting a bloody nose."[122] Her eyeglasses may have become broken in this bit of "horseplay." The details surrounding this event are vague in police and news reports. It appears this incident went beyond a little roughhousing and, given Connie's bloody nose and broken eyeglasses, another ice pack might have been in order.

Connie's tent-mates left for breakfast but Connie decided to stay behind. She told them she was going to return the ice pack to the dispensary. Instead of heading to the dispensary, and without having eaten breakfast that morning, Connie left the ice pack on her bunk bed and proceeded to walk off the camp grounds onto Indian Mountain Road. Carol Baker, the tent's group leader, learned she was missing after the other tent-mates returned from breakfast. August Epp was the caretaker at Camp Sloane and between 7:55 A.M. and 8:15 A.M. he was driving the camp truck, accompanied by Julius "Buckshot" Dennis, north on Indian Mountain Road. He noticed a girl walk out the camp driveway and head north on the same road. Epp thought she must have been one of the camp counselors and didn't pay any more attention to her.

Around 9:15 A.M., Mary Robinson, the Girls Camp Director, told some workers that Connie was missing. The staff immediately searched the camp. August Epp, recognizing the description of Connie as being the girl he saw earlier, jumped into his personal car and drove the nearby roads searching for her. He drove up Indian Mountain Road onto Route 44 toward Lakeville center, and south on Route 41 (Lakeville-Sharon Road) and back to Camp Sloane. He saw no sign of Connie, nor had any of the searchers back at the camp.

As a result of the local search conducted by Camp Sloane personnel, Connie wasn't reported missing to the police for several hours. It is possible that Camp Director Ernest Roberts wanted to avoid the negative publicity that would occur when word spread that one of his campers was missing. And, given his experiences with the state police and the health department years before, he was probably hesitant to be in the eye of another investigation.

Camp Sloane Tent Cabin in the 1950s
Unidentified Camper
Author's Collection

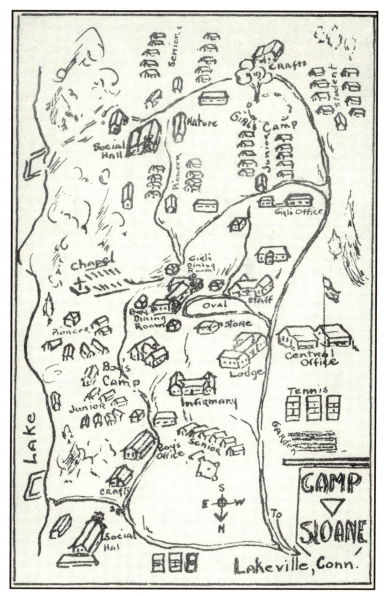

Undated Postcard Map of Camp Sloane
Connie's tent was located in the Junior Girls section of the camp (upper right)
Author's Collection

MICHAEL C. DOOLING

After thoroughly searching the camp for Connie, Roberts had no option but to call for assistance. Finally, at 11:30 A.M. "Gov." Roberts made the call to the Connecticut State Police. Trooper Richard Chapman was the first to respond. State police from the Canaan barracks immediately instituted a search of the local area and continued until 3:40 P.M., when they determined this was not simply a lost girl. At that time, police alerted radio stations and newspapers about Connie's disappearance. The next day, a 13-state alarm was issued and search teams led by Captain Paul Lavin and Lieutenant Osmus Avery scoured the woods surrounding the camp but had no luck finding her. Trooper Chapman checked local railroad stations, taxi services and bus companies to determine if Connie had been seen by ticket agents or drivers. No one had seen her but all promised to be on the alert for her.

Trooper Richard Chapman

In 1952, the Connecticut State Police was considered a state-of-the-art law enforcement agency. Founded in 1903 with five members, it had grown to more than 300 officers, including twelve women, ten resident troopers and several detectives. Eleven barracks covered the state and troopers were primarily involved in patrolling the state's growing network of roads and highways. Edward J. Hickey, Commissioner of State Police, was highly respected and had revamped the department since he took over in 1939. He had established the first state police FM three-way mobile communications network in the country with over 360 units, substantially increased the size of the department, and had updated the Bureau of Identification – the forerunner to the modern forensics laboratory. The department headquarters housed the detective division, fingerprinting and photograph units, radio and teletype communications, police training activities, a fire marshal and an emergency division.

At the time Connie disappeared, the Connecticut State Police Department was annually processing more than 16,000 criminal complaints with over 3,000 criminal arrests and more than 11,000 motor vehicle arrests in addition to some 27,000 warnings. The fingerprint division had close to 100,000 sets of fingerprints on file and made over 4,000 identifications using fingerprint comparisons in a single year. The department also maintained a "rogues gallery" of photographs of known criminals numbering over 38,000 images. The communications division handled 150,000 teletype calls annually, more than half of which were broadcasts from other states. Upon the department's fiftieth anniversary in 1953, Governor John Lodge praised the department as being "second to none."[123] Perhaps in 1946, the state of Vermont wasn't prepared to handle the Paula Welden disappearance, but the State of Connecticut had considerable resources at its disposal and extensive experience to bear on such a case.

The Connecticut State Police distributed a missing person circular describing Connie's physical description to policemen and others involved in the search for her. It was also sent to law enforcement agencies in neighboring states. It read in part:

> Connie Smith, 10 years old, 5 feet tall, weight approximately 85 pounds. Her eyes are blue, she has shoulder-length brown hair with bangs, and is very suntanned. Fingernails are unusually long and well cared for for a youngster. Has a slight, almost

imperceptible scar under her right nostril. Her upper "eye" teeth are just coming in. She has flat feet and her arms are unusually long. Connie is near-sighted and when reading or writing gets very close to her work. She had glasses but they were broken while she was at camp.

She loves all animals, especially horses; likes to swim and is a fair swimmer; likes to color with crayons and read funny books; makes friends very easily with youngsters; can handle a baton but is not very good at it; and has a vivid imagination especially about her animal friends – some of her creations are about a rattlesnake pet and her horse "Toni" (a white mare) that can twirl a baton.

Although Connie was but ten-years-old she was tall for her age; some people said she could have passed for twelve or thirteen. This observation was supported by the caretaker when he mistook her for a camp counselor. On the morning of her disappearance, Connie was dressed in a bright red windbreaker, blue shorts with a plaid cuff, brown bandana halter top, tan shoes and a red hair ribbon. Investigators believed she carried no extra clothes, food or money, though she may have been carrying a black zippered purse containing photographs of friends.

The well-known photograph of Connie that appeared on the missing person posters was taken by Paul Parker, a photographer hired by the camp. A week before Connie disappeared, he had taken photos of all the campers and their tent-mates. The "mug-shot" image printed on missing person circulars didn't reflect Connie's true temperament. She may not have been happy at camp that day or perhaps the group photograph was taken before she had a chance to smile. Another photograph, taken in happier times, portrays a much happier girl with an engaging smile.

Connecticut State Troopers stopped cars along Route 44 up to the New York border hoping to find someone who saw something. In 1952, Route 44 was a major artery crossing the entire state of Connecticut. It started in Plymouth, Massachusetts, crossed Rhode Island and Connecticut, and continued into New York through Ulster and Dutchess counties. It offered travelers and truckers convenient access to four states in the days before the interstate highway system.

Police also interviewed scores of residents in searching for Connie. The interviews helped them trace her movements that morning toward the center of Lakeville where her trail disappeared. According to Lieutenant Osmun Avery, Connie maintained "considerable independence"[124] that morning and had stopped twice to inquire about the way to the village center. After August Epp saw her along the road near the camp entrance, she was seen about 8:00 A.M. by Mr. & Mrs. Hobbs Horstman who were taking their morning walk. As they walked south on Indian Mountain Road toward Camp Sloane, they saw a young girl walking in the opposite direction – toward Lakeville. They passed one another about halfway between Camp Sloane and Route 112 (Interlaken Road).

Next, she was seen by Mrs. Alice Walsh who lived at the intersection of Route 112 and Indian Mountain Road, about a quarter of a mile from the camp entrance. Mrs. Walsh told police the girl stopped at her home to ask directions to Lakeville, which she gave her. She noticed the girl had tears in her eyes and appeared to have been crying. As Connie left, Mrs. Adams watched her walk up the hill toward Lakeville. Mrs. Walsh later commented, "At the time she seemed old enough to be out on her own."[125] Connie proceeded up Indian Mountain Road, crossed Interlaken Road and continued toward Route 44 (Millerton Road). Connie again stopped for directions at the home of Frederick L. Cadman about 8:15 A.M. Two women there provided her with directions and watched her walk out the driveway and continue to head toward Lakeville. Both times Connie inquired about directions, she was near the intersection of another road. Lieutenant Avery stated, "She was insistent on knowing the way to Lakeville."[126] These witnesses helped state police determine she was heading in an easterly direction.

Around 8:30 A.M., a married couple, Mr. and Mrs. John Brun, were on their way to their upholstery shop in Lakeville. They were driving along Route 44 from their home in the village of Millerton, New York, when they saw Connie Smith. The police reported, "As they approached the area of the Belgo Rd. and Route 44 intersection they observed a girl on the south portion of the highway (Rte. #44) hitch-hiking a ride toward Lakeville. They slowed down and intended to give the girl a ride, however, Mr. Brun who was driving the car, decided against it."[127] The couple remarked to one another that "their daughter was about the same age and how awful it was for a young girl like that to be bumming a ride."[128] They continued on their way to Lakeville and didn't think about that moment of indecision until they saw in the newspaper that a camper had disappeared.

Lakeville Center in the 1950s
Author's Collection

Others observed Connie in the same vicinity about 8:45 A.M. Mrs. Frank Barnett, who lived on Belgo Road, saw Connie walking on the north side of Route 44 near Belgo Road heading east toward Lakeville center.[129] Unfortunately, it isn't clear in the police files what her vantage point was – whether she was walking nearby, looking out a window of her house, standing on her property or driving an automobile.

The Bruns claimed they had seen Connie on the south side of the road heading east, which was with the direction of the traffic heading toward Lakeville. Yet Mrs. Barnett claimed Connie was walking on the north side of the road still heading toward Lakeville but against traffic. If Mrs. Barnett's observation was accurate, Connie may have crossed the road and was walking toward a vehicle (perhaps out of Mrs. Barnett's view) that had stopped to give her a lift. The vehicle would either have been heading west (away from Lakeville) on Route 44 near Belgo Road (which intersects on the north side of Route 44), or it may have been heading west and pulled into the entrance to Belgo Road so as to be off the main traffic artery, or it could have been entering Route 44 from Belgo Road. Connie had been walking and hitchhiking for close to 45 minutes and may have viewed any vehicle that stopped, even one going in the opposite direction, as being helpful. The driver may have engaged her in conversation about where she was headed and may well have offered to take her where she wanted to go in spite of the direction the vehicle was facing.

The sightings by the Bruns couple and Mrs. Barnett placed Connie farther east than previously thought. Belgo Road is only about a half mile from Lakeville center, but about $1^1/_2$ miles from Camp Sloane. About 45 minutes had passed since she left the camp grounds. Whether Connie walked the entire distance or managed to thumb a ride to Belgo Road is uncertain, but no one came forward saying they had given her a ride. The timing is such that it seems likely she walked the entire distance. On July 18th, Lieutenant Avery announced, "One new clue placed the missing girl about half a mile farther east along Route 44...Beyond that we have nothing new as to her possible whereabouts."[130] Mrs. Barnett was the last person known to have seen Connie alive.

There were a few other possible sightings the day Connie disappeared. About 9:00 A.M., Judge William Raynsford of Salisbury saw two girls walking along Route 44 toward Lakeville but coming from the east. When interviewed, he speculated to Trooper Chapman that Connie might have been thrown over a wall or into a culvert along Route 44. This prompted Chapman and several highway workers to search every culvert and drain basin in the area. That afternoon, a young woman from Sharon, Connecticut saw a girl in a white shirt and blue-striped shorts walking near the woods on Lime Rock Road. She called to her but the girl went back into the woods. Although the girl's clothing didn't match those that Connie was wearing, the state police still searched the woods but found no sign of her. Another woman saw a girl fitting Connie's description wearing a red garment and riding in a large, milk tank truck between 5:00 and 6:00 P.M. Milk haulers in the area were canvassed but nothing came of the report. None of those sightings could be corroborated, but every single one that was reported was investigated.

The ground search was expanded on July 18th and state troopers used United States Geological Survey maps to ensure they didn't miss any small streets, logging roads or trails. They looked into more wells, culverts, and drain basins, and dragged some with a hook; explored abandoned buildings, cellars and old dumps; and searched lakes, swamps, water-filled mines and reservoirs. Lieutenant Avery announced an airplane had been assigned to search for the missing girl. Trooper Robert Harrison piloted a Connecticut state police plane; by his side was Trooper Chapman as an observer.

Clueless in New England

The plane was joined by an air-sea rescue plane from Westover Field, Massachusetts, and by three planes flown by the Connecticut Wing of the Civil Air Patrol from the Winsted area. The airplanes crisscrossed the terrain surrounding Lakeville, about twenty miles in area, including portions of Massachusetts and New York State. They flew along roads, railroad tracks and river banks. Observers peered intently with binoculars and the naked eye as they flew over woods, lakes, old iron quarries and farmland looking for any sign of Connie. At one point, they spotted a white flag flying on top of a tree, causing a few minutes of hope. The pilot radioed searchers on the ground and they determined the flag had been placed there as a marker for gypsy moth spraying. Connie was nowhere to be seen.

Two days after her disappearance, Connie's father arrived in Connecticut from Sundance, Wyoming, to take part in the search. Smith reminded Trooper Chapman of the "Marlboro Man." "He was wearing a 10-gallon hat and dungarees and that was back before dungarees were popular."[131] After Mr. Smith arrived, more air searches were conducted and included airplanes and helicopters. Connie's father flew over the area searching for his daughter in a plane he had chartered at the Great Barrington Airport in Massachusetts. The aircraft flew low over the entire area in an effort to spot Connie but the summer foliage made it difficult to see into the wooded areas. Mr. Smith called off the air search as it appeared to be a fruitless exercise. Connie's father also searched in the woods on horseback. Back home in Wyoming, Connie was accustomed to camping out on the family ranch. Mr. Smith thought it was possible she had attempted to do the same in the Connecticut hills. He found nothing.

Connie's mother also arrived shortly after learning of the disappearance. She had been staying with her mother, Mrs. Carl Jensen of Greenwich, for the summer and she had visited her daughter at Camp Sloane three days prior to her disappearance. She was hopeful Connie may have gone to visit family friends. Mrs. Smith contacted several of them who lived in Massachusetts in hopes that Connie would find her way to one of their homes. Mrs. Smith spent two days in the search area and then returned to Greenwich so she would be fairly close by. Camp officials said Connie was "highly self-reliant and independent,"[132] but group leader Carol Baker stated she seemed somewhat homesick after her mother had visited. She may have attempted to go into town to use the telephone to call one of her parents. The nearest phone, located in the camp office, was off limits to campers except in emergencies.

Authorities theorized she may have attempted to return home to Sundance. Relatives and friends in Ohio, Illinois, Indiana, Nebraska, and North Dakota were notified to be on the lookout and police departments along the route to Wyoming were alerted. At one point Peter Smith flew to Chicago in hopes Connie might have gone there to visit relatives.

The state police considered the possibility of some sort of parental involvement in Connie's disappearance, perhaps one of them abducting her in order to see her more than the divorce decree allowed. Trooper Chapman recalled this possibility ten years later. "I never saw Connie Smith in my life. But I grew to know her – her personality traits, her likes and dislikes. I also got to know her parents: they were both fine people. I think the sincerity of the father impressed me most."[133]

The search grew dramatically in size and scope. Detective Sergeant Russell Starks of the Canaan Barracks said that the Connie Smith disappearance was the largest missing person search in his memory. Connecticut State Police sent teletype messages to law enforcement officials in the Northeast, the Midwest and the West. Newspapers and radio stations throughout the Northeast cooperated with investigators by notifying readers and listeners to be on the lookout for Connie on the chance she might be hitchhiking through the area. Her photograph and description were printed in newspapers and a fledgling television station in New Haven broadcast her image to its viewers. During the month following Connie's disappearance, the local weekly newspaper, *The Lakeville Journal*, carried only two brief articles about the case. The reason why the local newspaper chose not to give more coverage to this national story is unclear. Perhaps since Connie was a camper from out of town, the editor may have felt her story didn't deserve the coverage that might have been granted to a ten-year-old daughter of a local resident. A summer camp run by an out-of-state organization, populated with a bunch of out-of-town kids, wasn't really a part of the fabric of Lakeville nor its concern.

Fortunately, the story was carried by other state and national newspapers. The wide coverage resulted in dozens of reports that needed to be tracked down by police investigators. Connie was "sighted" in several different locales. All those leads proved false. A New York woman told police she had seen a girl matching Connie's description among gypsies camped on the outskirts of Amenia. New York State Police investigated a motor van being driven by the gypsies. They were mostly from Arkansas and worked as itinerant barn painters and crop harvesters. Police found no indication Connie was traveling with them. Mrs. Alfred Nicholls of Northville, Connecticut reported she thought she saw Connie in Cooperstown, New York. She had seen a young girl fitting Connie's description and wearing a red gabardine jacket even though the weather was warm. Cooperstown police checked all museums and hotels and found no evidence that Connie had been there.

State police paid particular attention to old quarries and abandoned iron mines that dot the area around Lakeville. Most of them date from colonial days and were closed long ago. One large water-filled pit was less than a half mile off the Lakeville-Millerton road; police kept an eye on this in case Connie had fallen into the water and drowned. Her body would surface within a few days if she had met this fate. No body ever surfaced.

State Police Commander Lieutenant Avery was as frustrated as everyone else. His men had scoured the entire area around Lakeville as thoroughly as possible. If Connie wasn't in that area she could be anywhere. After three weeks, the investigation had hit a stone wall and the frustrated commander stated, "We'll just have to wait for something to turn up…We've had nothing tangible on her whereabouts since then (when seen at Belgo Road)…We've done about all we can except find the girl. Police departments throughout the country have been sent circulars asking to be on the lookout for Connie. We've run down tips which were as much as two weeks old. But we'll keep trying."[134]

After months of dead end leads, the ground search for Connie Smith intensified that autumn. Connecticut game wardens, who conducted daily patrols in the Connecticut woods during hunting season, were instructed to be on the lookout for Connie. State police provided all game wardens with the missing person circular describing the missing girl, in hopes they might run across her body. An anonymous caller to the state police suggested Connie may have been murdered and her corpse buried in a freshly dug grave on top of a coffin containing someone else's body. Using a steel rod, Trooper Chapman probed the graves of people who had died in the weeks prior to Connie's disappearance. Police even gathered scat from wild animals and had it analyzed to determine if it contained any sign of human remains. The state police again searched the area from the air, a task made easier with the foliage off the trees. A new missing person bulletin was issued by the state police to every police department in the United States, the FBI, private detective agencies, optical journals, dental journals, and all school superintendents in Connecticut. A reward was announced and Commissioner Hickey had the check in his hands. Mrs. Smith offered a $3,000 reward if

Connie was found alive before January 1, 1954, and $1,000 if her body was recovered before that date.

Helen Smith wrote to the *Hartford Courant*, appealing to local hunters to look for and retrieve any clothing they might encounter in the woods. "I could recognize anything of hers. I can't believe that's what happened to her, though (getting lost in the woods). She knew the woods too well." She pleaded, "Christmas was always such a big event at our house. This year I feel I can't stand it. They say time heals everything – but not this. Each day is a little harder to face. We all know we might lose our children. But not to know what happened to her isn't human. Please do all you can."[135]

In late November, eighteen members of the Connecticut Trail Riders Association searched for Connie Smith's body. Arriving the night before, they stabled their horses at Lucy Drummond's Stock Farm in Salisbury. Horsemen from Granby, Collinsville, Simsbury, New Haven, Wethersfield, Hartford and Somers participated in the search and attempted to "cover the roads and trails wherever passable in an area from the New York – Conn. State lines to a point easterly to the Twin Lakes and southerly from the Mass. – Conn. line to Route 112."[136] Hampered by icy trails, three groups of six riders each searched Mount Riga, Mount Washington and Red Mountain. The search parties covered over a sixteen square mile area of brush and woodlands yet their efforts proved fruitless.

The quest to find Connie took some odd twists the following year. A 27-year-old horse named "Lady Wonder" in Richmond, Virginia, with a reputation for being clairvoyant, gave the next direction in the case. Lady used a crude typewriter of sorts and poked letters with her nose to spell out messages. The horse had the reputation of being able to answer mathematical problems, foretell the gender of an unborn child, and predict the future. Lady Wonder's owner, Mrs. Claudia Fonda, charged one dollar for three questions.

MICHAEL C. DOOLING

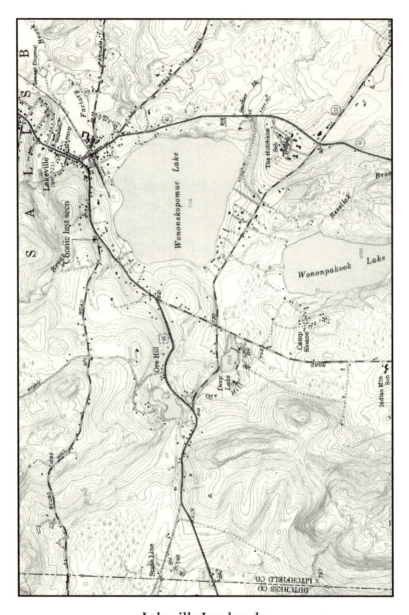

Lakeville Landmarks
USGS Map, Sharon (Conn.) Quadrangle, 1950

CLUELESS IN NEW ENGLAND

In December 1952, Lady Wonder was employed in the search for 4-year-old Danny Matson of Quincy, Mass. When a family friend asked Lady Wonder about the whereabouts of the boy who had been missing since January 1951, she spelled out "Pittsfield Water Wheel." When detectives searched around Pittsfield, Mass., they found nothing. Then police played with the message the horse had pointed out and thought she may have been off slightly and they re-interpreted the message "Pit field wilde water," which

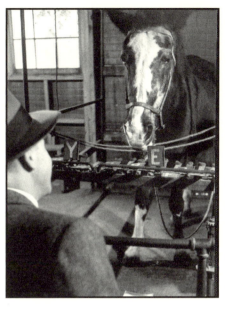

Lady Wonder & "Typewriter"
Life Magazine, December 1, 1950
Getty Images

they believed referred to the abandoned water-filled Field-Wilde Quarry in Quincy. When the police drained the water from the quarry they found Danny's remains. Massachusetts officials were at a loss as to how to explain the phenomenon. District Attorney Edmund R. Dewing admitted it was the horse that provided the clue to finding the missing boy and said, "It's stranger than fiction. And we kept it a complete secret because we didn't want people to think we were completely out of our minds."[137]

Nine months after Connie's disappearance, Peter Smith was desperate for any type of help in the case and went to Richmond to seek assistance from Lady Wonder. Helen Smith later reflected, "We were ready to try anything. We'd tried everything else we could think of."[138] Lady Wonder directed Smith to look in Los

Angeles for his daughter, which he did. Armed with 10,000 missing person circulars, he connected with police and reporters and tried his best to find her. While there, he even appeared on a national television show, *House Party* hosted by Art Linkletter, and made an impassioned plea for help from the public. Unfortunately, Lady Wonder's success at clairvoyance was sporadic and failed to provide a meaningful clue in the Connie Smith case.

In early April 1953, a traveling jewelry salesman named Frederick W. Pope walked into the police station at Washington Court House, Ohio, and related a bizarre story about Connie Smith. Pope told the police that he and a traveling companion named Jack Walker had picked up Connie Smith when she was hitchhiking along Route 44. They drove her to Arizona where she was strangled by Walker during an argument. A few hours after her death, Pope beat Walker with an iron bar when he was changing a flat tire. Walker died from his injuries. Pope said he buried both bodies in Arizona and offered to show police the location of the two graves.

Connie's parents wanted the police to go to Arizona with Pope to look for the grave. Her father said, "If she is dead and this man knows where the grave is, we want to know it. If he's just a screwball, we want to know that too."[139] Major Leo Carroll of the Connecticut State Police conducted a telephone interview with Pope. After writing twelve pages summarizing the interview he noted, "He's a rascal! He's a rascal if he did it; and he's a rascal if he didn't."[140] At one point Pope was interviewed by a reporter from the *Hartford Courant* over the telephone. When asked why he picked up Connie Smith he responded, "She was just another girl. We done a lot of foolish things before. We picked up girls all along the road. We met them in taverns or anywhere." The summary of the interview was printed in the *Hartford Courant*[141] describing more details:

Clueless in New England

Pope said he and Walker had spent the night of July 15-16 at Pawtucket, RI where they picked up a girl named Wilma Sames, wife of a navy man. They were traveling in a stolen car and several times changed license plates. On a road near Salisbury they saw Connie Smith hitchhiking, he said, and picked her up. Pope said the girl told them she wanted to return to her father in Wyoming and mentioned something about a fall at camp.

The quartet drove to New York, where Pope said Walker bought some clothes for the girl, and then headed West. He estimates they were on the road five or six days, and slept in the car instead of motels. He said the Sames girl left them in Oklahoma, when Walker gave her $22 to buy a bus ticket to Texas.

The two men and the girl continued on to Arizona, and at a fork in the road the girl told Walker he was heading the wrong way. An argument resulted, and Pope said he got out of the car and started walking. About 45 minutes later Walker drove up and announced he had killed the girl and now the two would have to bury her.

Pope said they buried her near a construction pit somewhere between Show Low and Carrizo, Ariz. It was along U.S. 60. Both men were drinking. They drove on about 30 miles until they began quarreling and had a flat tire between Florence Junction and Superior, Ariz. Pope said he beat Walker to death with a tire tool while the repair was being made, and later dumped the body into a side road ravine and pulled down rocks and an overhanging shelf to cover it.

When pressed to describe Connie's appearance, Pope had difficulty. He didn't remember the length of her hair or the color of her jacket, nor could he remember the name of any town in Connecticut, nor the names of any of the Arizona hotels where he claimed to have lodged. He blamed his bad memory on having been drunk a good deal of the time during his cross-country trip. Pope had previously confessed to the murder of a man named "Bill." Four years earlier, he told St. Louis police he had murdered the man, an acquaintance, and burned his body on a beach in Los Angeles. The police in that city knew nothing of such a murder and had no interest in Pope.

Law enforcement officials in Arizona began proceedings to issue a murder warrant. They planned to fly Pope to Arizona to show them where the bodies of Walker and Connie Smith were buried. Although authorities in both states were dubious about the story, Connecticut State Police Detective Russell Starks was dispatched to Ohio to question the man. On April 8, 1953, Detective Starks questioned Pope for nine hours. He questioned him continually from 9:00 A.M. to 3:00 P.M. and started again at 8:00 P.M. Gradually, Pope's story disintegrated. Three hours later, Pope broke down sobbing and exclaimed, "It's all wrong! It's all a hoax."[142] Several things didn't support his story. Authorities determined there was no navy man named Sames stationed in Rhode Island at the time. More importantly, Pope had in his possession a card from the Indiana Employment Security Division in Indianapolis that he obtained when he registered there to find work. It was dated July 15, 1952 – the day before Connie disappeared.

Frederick Pope claimed he first got the idea for confessing to the crime after seeing a missing persons posting in a post office in Waco, Texas. He obtained more information when he watched the television show, Art Linkletter's *House Party*, which had just gone on the air on September 1, 1952. Peter Smith appeared on the show appealing to all of America to be on the lookout for his daughter. Pope learned from Peter Smith's appearance specific details relating to Connie's physical characteristics, her father's affection for her and other details that weren't printed on the missing person circulars. He also noticed on *House Party* how tall Connie's father was and told police that Connie frequently mentioned her father's height. This led police to believe he had at least spoken to the girl. Pope, a former mental patient and an alcoholic, claimed he lied about the murders to get out of circulation and to get re-admitted to a hospital. It's possible that Pope's companion Jack Walker was nothing more than his nickname for a companion of a different sort - Johnnie Walker® Scotch Whisky.

State Police Commissioner Edward J. Hickey, who had guided the Connecticut State Police into a modern police force, died of leukemia while in office on September 22, 1953. The Smith case had haunted Hickey, and before his death he issued a plea to his troopers. He wrote, "I am not satisfied that this girl or any other young girl can disappear from the face of the earth for any long period, remain alive, and forsake all friendships. Dig a bit deeper in this case. Go into the woods again and go deeper; search the waterways again and don't take anything for granted. We want the answer to Connie Smith's disappearance."[143] Unfortunately, no amount of further effort would find her.

The tempest swirling around Connie's disappearance was only matched three years after she disappeared when the state of Connecticut was walloped by two hurricanes, one with a strangely familiar name. Hurricane Connie struck on August 13, 1955, pouring up to six inches of rain on the state. Five days later, Hurricane Diane dumped 14 inches of water in 30 hours. Then the floods came. On the morning of August 19, much of western Connecticut was flooded by rivers and streams overflowing their banks. Amidst the washed out roads, disrupted utilities and services, and clean-up efforts during the weeks that followed, a man called the state police – collect – from Canada to get something off his chest regarding Connie Smith. The man identified himself as William Dugan and said he had worked for a circus in Hartford thirteen years earlier. Perhaps he had miscalculated the years and also planned to confess to starting a catastrophic fire in a circus tent in Hartford in 1944 that killed 167 people. The state trooper and Dugan agreed to meet in Canada the next day but the statewide problems resulting from the floods prevented the trooper from leaving. Instead, he asked Canadian police to meet with the man. The Canadian police didn't call back and the matter wasn't pursued again. The state police interviewed Dugan's ex-wife and discovered William Dugan was an American soldier then stationed in Japan. The caller's true identity was never determined.

Trooper Leo Turcotte accepted the collect call from the man who called himself William Dugan in 1955 and he continued to work on this angle even after his retirement. He ran across the name of a William Henry Redmond who had murdered eight-year-old Jane Marie Althoff in Trainer, Pennsylvania in 1951. Redmond had strangled Jane Marie at the Penn-Premier Show Carnival where he worked running a Ferris wheel. He left her body in the back of a truck on the carnival grounds and his fingerprints were found in the cab of the truck. Redmond disappeared immediately after the murder. Police believed he had spent some time in Canada and caught up with him in Nebraska in 1988. Connecticut State Police investigated the man but could not determine if he was ever in Connecticut in the 1950s. While in jail awaiting his trial, Redmond told another inmate he had committed four murders in all but had only gotten caught for one. Redmond was very ill and never went to trial, but before he died he submitted to a polygraph test. When questioned about Connie Smith's disappearance, he denied any involvement and passed the lie detector test.

Clueless in New England

Frederick Pope was not the only man to confess to killing Connie Smith. In 1957, George J. Davies was arrested for slaying two girls in Connecticut. One of them was sixteen-year-old Gaetane Boivin of Waterbury, who had advertised in a local newspaper looking for a housekeeping position. Her family had moved down from Canada three years earlier and settled in Waterbury. In her classified ad[144] she tried to take advantage of her French Canadian heritage:

> **Situations Wanted - Female**
> **FRENCH GIRL** – Desires light house-
> keeping by day, or mother's helper.
> Plaza 4-5748 or 52 Cherry St.

Davies, a resident of Thomaston, read the newspaper that morning over coffee at the Waldorf Cafeteria in downtown Waterbury. He was perusing the employment ads and was attracted to the advertisement. He called the telephone number and Gaetane answered. He told her he wanted her to do some housework for him and set up an appointment to pick her up at her home at 9:30 A.M. Boivin wasn't heard from again after she left her home that day.

A few days later, on May 12th, nine-year-old Brenda Jane Doucette of Town Line Road in Bristol was walking to school along a secluded road on her way to Fall Mountain School. Davies picked up the blue-eyed, blonde third-grader in his car, drove her to a secluded dead end road and sexually assaulted her. When she resisted and screamed he choked her with a green sweater, leaving it wrapped around her neck, and then stabbed her twenty-two times with a screwdriver; three of those wounds pierced her heart. After two days of searching by more than 100 volunteers, Brenda Jane's body was found in the nearby town of Wolcott in a clump of bushes about 200 feet off a rarely used back-road off Allentown Road.

It wasn't until May 21st that Gaetane Boivin's remains were

found by a hunter along a secluded stretch of Greystone Road in the Bucks Hill section of Waterbury. Davies had kept his appointment with Gaetane on May 9th and once he identified himself as the caller she willingly got into his car believing she was going to clean his house. Davies drove her to the Mattatuck State Forest in Waterbury, stopped along Greystone Road and assaulted her in the front seat of his car. When she resisted him and slapped him in the face, he grabbed her throat and choked her for several minutes. He then stabbed her fifty times with a screwdriver, thirty of the stab wounds in the region of the heart. He drove about a half mile down an almost impassable, abandoned portion of Greystone Road and pushed her body out the door into a ditch.

After he was arrested for murder, George Davies, age 38, was questioned at length about Connie Smith's disappearance. He denied any involvement whatsoever. The father of three had previously been arrested in 1952 for sexually molesting two young girls in Thomaston, for which he was sentenced to a three-year prison term. He was released after a year and a day. After his 1952 arrest, he was questioned extensively by State Police Sergeant Wilbur Calkins about the Smith case. Davies claimed he was working at the Lyons Garage in Thomaston at the time Connie Smith walked out of Camp Sloane and had nothing to do with her disappearance. According to time records kept by the garage's business manager, Davies worked from 8:00 A.M. to 6:00 P.M. the day Connie disappeared.[145] Davies' ex-wife confirmed this finding. Mrs. Davies had divorced George after his conviction for sexual molestation and was quite bitter. She told police she was on vacation from her job at the Seth Thomas Clock Company in Thomaston the week Connie disappeared. She used their only car that week and dropped her husband off at work at the garage in the morning and picked him up in the evening, validating his alibi.

Despite a plea of insanity at his trial, Davies was convicted and sentenced to the electric chair for the murder of Brenda Jane Doucette. Although he was indicted for the Boivin murder, that case didn't go to trial. Two years after he was arrested for the Boivin/Doucette murders and while he was sitting on death row in Wethersfield State Prison awaiting his fate, he decided to confess to not just one other murder but three. He claimed he murdered Jamila J. Martin of Waterbury, an unidentified woman in Watertown (whom he claimed he tortured and dumped into the Naugatuck River), and Connie Smith.

Connie's parents were notified of the development. Peter Smith told an Associated Press reporter, "He may be telling the truth, or he may just be trying to get off on an insanity plea. We just can't tell about this story. We just keep hoping. I've always felt my daughter is still alive somewhere. She would be 17 years old now, and she would be a tall girl, perhaps nearly six feet tall. We just keep hoping and praying."[146] The Smiths surely must have been torn in their emotions – hoping for closure in their daughter's disappearance after seven years and praying she hadn't been killed by this evil monster.

Law enforcement officials tried to determine if he could be connected to any of the crimes. The unidentified woman remained just that. No body was ever found and no missing person was reported that fit the circumstances. Another case held more promise. On April 22, 1957, Jamila Martin, age 26, had been found dead, fully clothed along a lonely stretch of Catering Road in Wolcott. Her body was found in a ditch near the entrance to a culvert about four feet below the level of the road. Even though her purse and belt were found on the opposite side of the road, it was determined that she had died from alcoholism and diabetic shock. Although there was a "slight trickle of blood from the mouth and a slight scratch on the nose"[147] there was no evidence of any violence and no foul play was suspected. The location of her body gave the appearance of having been dumped there from a car. Jamila was last seen by a friend in a tavern in Waterbury on Saturday at 4:30 P.M., but according to her brother had not been home in several days. Police learned that Jamila Martin and George Davies were acquainted with one another and may have been intimate at some point. Jamila's mother insisted her daughter and Davies had been out the night before, hitting various bars, and had left in Davies' car. Police could find no proof of her allegations, nor evidence of assault. They speculated she may have "suffered a fatal diabetic shock sometime Saturday night or Sunday and her body dumped by a panicky companion, who drove a car to the lonely stretch of road."[148] Despite the unusual circumstances of her death and Davies' confession, there was no indication that she died from anything other than natural causes.

Police investigators were more encouraged by Davies' possible association with the Connie Smith case. At one point, Davies was let out of prison briefly to show police where he buried Connie. Davies was fairly specific about where he buried her body. He said he buried her in a shallow grave about 10-15 feet up the bank of the Naugatuck River near Two Mile Bridge north of Thomaston. County Coroner John J. Casale believed if Davies buried her where he said, her remains probably washed away during the devastating flood that occurred in August 1955. Davies later changed his story and told the police he had lied about the burial location. Again he left the prison and guided investigators to a wooded area near Two Mile Bridge, away from the river, and pointed to a patch of ground about 15 feet square. In a secret agreement with the state police, the area was to be excavated after Davies was put to death a few days later. In exchange for providing the location of the grave-site, the police offered to accommodate his request to delay digging up the body. Davies told police he felt his disclosure would have a "shaming effect" on his children, as if conviction for the murder of an 8-year-old girl wasn't enough, and thought they would be better able to handle it after his execution.

During the evening of October 20, 1959, the State of Connecticut carried out the punishment imposed on George J. Davies. At 10:30 P.M., he was executed in the electric chair for the murder of Brenda Doucette. Half an hour before his execution, Davies confided to Lieutenant Wilbur Calkins that his confession to Connie Smith's murder had been a hoax all along.

The entire nation was watching for Connie Smith. Over the years, more than 200 alleged sightings were reported from around the country. Each one was investigated and none turned up anything. One of the better known sightings was from a photograph of a girl claiming to be an albino Indian from Quebec who had traveled to Fort Worth; the photo appeared in a September 1952 newspaper. Reports that she resembled Connie Smith came from two regions of the country - from a man in Louisiana and from a police chief in Wisconsin. The girl named Kim claimed she was from an Iroquois Indian tribe on the St. Regis River reservation between Canada and New York. She said she wanted to train horses in Texas, yet a rancher who took her in said she didn't know how to ride. The girl was not the missing camper.

Almost two years after Connie's disappearance, the *New York Journal American* printed a photograph of bathers on a beach in the Bronx. One of the girls pictured bore a resemblance to Connie Smith and was unidentified. When Peter Smith saw the photograph he thought it had a "marked resemblance"[149] to his daughter. The Connecticut State Police requested the newspaper run the photo again, this time asking the public if anyone recognized the girl. The girl's mother identified her and the matter was closed.

In 1962, the Connecticut State Police learned that the body of a young girl had been found near Flagstaff, Arizona in 1958. A postmortem examination determined the girl had died about a year earlier and Arizona police believed she had been murdered. She was between thirteen and seventeen years old and had teeth similar to Connie Smith's. Two dentists examined the X-rays of the teeth of the dead girl and compared them to those of Connie. They appeared to be almost identical, but after examination of all the remains the pathologist determined that the girl was not her. Had it been Connie, she would have been alive for five years after her disappearance.

The search for Connie Smith has been kept alive through newspapers, television and the Internet, and the publicity still generates leads. In 1988, a woman from Michigan saw a television segment about Connie's disappearance on *A Current Affair* and thought <u>she</u> might actually be Connie Smith. DNA testing determined she was not the long-lost Connie nor related to Peter Smith.

In 2002, a Litchfield woman formerly of Sandisfield, Massachusetts, read an anniversary article about the Connie Smith case in the *Waterbury Republican-American*. She had never heard the story before but something triggered a response. The woman remembered as a child that she, her five-year-old sister, and a nine-year-old friend had been scared by two men in a car during the same summer Connie disappeared. She recalled playing near a remote, dirt road when a green car drove up and two men tried to talk to them. An Italian looking man with a facial scar drove the car and said to them, "Are you playing, little girls?" Instinctively, the girls backed away. The men drove off only when another car pulled up in back of them. As the scar-faced man drove away, the girls memorized the license plate and turned it into a chant so they would remember it. The woman still remembered it: "QF–58–76, New York plate." She contacted the Waterbury *Republican-American*[150] and the Connecticut State Police. License plate records from that period are not well organized and were never entered into a database later on. The state police pursued the lead as best they could, as they had all the others, but could not identify the vehicle or its owner.

142

Clueless in New England

CONNECTICUT STATE POLICE DEPARTMENT

REWARD: $3,000.00 if found alive before Jan. 1, 1954

MISSING PERSON

REWARD: $1,000.00 for recovery of body before Jan. 1, 1954

Last seen July 16, 1952

Connie Smith, 10 years old, 5 feet tall, weight approximately 85 pounds. Her eyes are blue, she has shoulder-length brown hair with bangs, and is very suntanned. Fingernails are unusually long and well cared for for a youngster. Has a slight, almost imperceptible scar under her right nostril. Her upper "eye" teeth are just coming in. She has flat feet and her arms are unusually long. Connie is near-sighted and when reading or writing gets very close to her work. She had glasses but they were broken while she was at camp.

She loves all animals, especially horses; likes to swim and is a fair swimmer; likes to color with crayons and read funny books; makes friends very easily with youngsters; can handle a baton but is not very good at it; and has a vivid imagination, especially about her animal friends - some of her creations are about a rattlesnake pet and her horse "Toni" (a white mare) that can twirl a baton.

Connie Smith

Connie Smith has been missing from Camp Sloane, Indian Mountain Road, Salisbury, Connecticut since 8:00 a.m. July 16, 1952. This girl had been injured in a fall at the camp on July 15, but to all appearances her injuries were not serious. She was examined at the camp dispensary and given an ice pack to hold on her hip. The last conversation which she had with the girls in her tent was that she was going to take the ice pack back to the dispensary. She did not go to the dispensary.

At about 8:30 a.m. Connie was seen trying to thumb a ride toward Lakeville, Conn. At the time she was on Route #44 about one half mile West of the Center of Lakeville. While going from the Camp to the point where she was last seen Connie had stopped at two houses to inquire the direction to Lakeville. It has been impossible to trace her beyond this point.

When last seen she was wearing navy blue shorts with a plaid cuff, bright red zipper long sleeved jacket, and tan leather shoes. Her hair was tied with a red ribbon. Name tags are in her clothes. She may have had a black zipper purse containing small pictures of friends. She had no extra clothes and no money.

She is the daughter of Helen Smith of Sundance, Wyoming and Peter Smith of Newcastle, Wyoming. Mrs. Smith's father is Carl C. Jensen of Greenwich, Conn., telephone Greenwich 8-1665. Connie has lived on a ranch in Wyoming most of her life, is a leader among children and is self-reliant. This was her first time at a camp and she was to return to Wyoming in one month. While she seemed to like camp she was a little homesick after a visit from her mother on July 13. Connie's paternal grandparents are Ex-Governor and Mrs. Nels. H. Smith, Sundance, Wy.

If you have any information please contact by telephone or telegram collect Commissioner Edward J. Hickey, Connecticut State Police Department, 100 Washington Street, Hartford 1, Connecticut, Telephone number Hartford 5-0181.

(OVER) CASE NO. B-57-H

Missing Person Circular for Connie Smith
Courtesy of the Salisbury Historical Society

Connie's parents remained optimistic even after all the searching revealed nothing. They expressed the hope that the fall Connie experienced the day before she disappeared could have caused amnesia and that the girl couldn't remember who she was or where she came from. Helen Smith told the newspaper that in the fall Connie not only hurt her hip but also bumped her head. "Just before she walked out of the camp and disappeared, Connie told her roommates she was going to take an ice pack to the infirmary. But when I arrived later that day, the ice pack was still on her bunk. To me that proves something had happened to her mind."[151] Peter Smith told the newspaper what he had learned about amnesia, "The history of amnesia cases is that sometimes it takes a year or two to regain memory. We hope some day we will find her. If people will only be on the watch for any new girl that has come into town, or a girl who can't recall too much of her past, maybe they will spot her."[152]

Richard Chapman, the first trooper on the scene at Camp Sloane, became Sergeant and took charge of the photographic division of the Connecticut State Police Bureau of Identification. He retired in 1976 after twenty-four years on the force. When he was interviewed in 1974, Chapman expressed his thoughts about the case. He believed Connie had been picked up by someone driving by, murdered, and her body buried or dumped in one of the water-filled iron quarries in the area. "She was picked up by someone in a car, I'm sure this is what happened. Some day I'm going to find Connie Smith and identify her. But whether we'll ever identify the perpetrators, I have my doubts."[153]

In Connecticut, unsolved cases involving missing persons and capital crimes are never closed. Connecticut State Police Detective Karoline Keith is now assigned to the Connie Smith case and has been for several years. Periodically, leads come to her attention and she, like the troopers and detectives who worked on the case for many decades before her, follows up every one of them. Although Detective Keith doubts that Connie is still alive she is hopeful her remains may eventually be found.

In the Paula Welden and Connie Smith cases, nearly every known trail, both literal and figurative, was followed in attempting to find these two young women. Land, air and boat searches, attempts to track down cars and trucks in the vicinity, and interviews with witnesses were all executed diligently. Sightings in distant towns, clairvoyants that gave false hope, statements from drunks, and confessions of criminals were all investigated. Yet, not one clue emerged in either case that led authorities to any conclusions. "Foul play" is the generally accepted theory in both cases. Although there is as little evidence of that possibility as any other, it seems to be the most probable explanation.

Though it occurred two states away, the disappearance of Connie Smith is similar in circumstances to the Paula Welden case – a trusting female, walking and hitchhiking along a road, and disappearing as though someone never wanted her found. If there was a chance the two cases had a common element, such as both young women being abducted and killed by the same person, it seemed logical there might be other cases of a similar nature. If one draws a circle connecting Bennington and Lakeville a large geographic area is defined encompassing Albany, New York to the west and Northampton, Massachusetts to the east. Searching old newspapers for other women who disappeared within this circle soon brought another case out of the shadows. This disappearance from a few years earlier was much less publicized but also involved a young, female hitchhiker. The whole story sounded remarkably familiar.

Chapter IV

"...the third time it's enemy action."
Ian Fleming, *Goldfinger*

Michael C. Dooling

Katherine Hull
Courtesy of The Berkshire Eagle

CLUELESS IN NEW ENGLAND

West Mountain

At first glance, the disappearances of Paula Welden and Connie Smith seem to be totally independent events. They vanished in two different states, in towns approximately 86 miles apart, and were not only separated by distance but also by the passage of more than six years between their disappearances. The similarity between the two cases was mentioned in an Associated Press article published in several newspapers two weeks after Connie disappeared. "The disappearance of Connie Smith was at least as puzzling, if not more so, than that of Paula Welden of Stamford."[154] This appears to be the only published comparison of the two cases and it did not appear to influence the Smith investigators to consider a possible connection. Apparently, the passage of time and the fact that the two cases had occurred two states away from one another precluded any investigation into their similarities. Events in Lakeville, Connecticut seemed too far removed from those in Bennington, Vermont to matter to investigators.

The Paula Welden – Connie Smith cases were not only differentiated geographically and temporally, but also by the ages of the victims. Paula was eighteen and Connie just ten years old, though Connie was described many times as looking older than her age. She was taller than most ten-year-old girls and several people said she could be mistaken for a girl a few years older. In spite of the differences, there are several important similarities between the two disappearances. The two had permanent residences out-of-state and were only temporarily living in the towns where they vanished. Both intentionally left the relative safety of a college campus or a summer camp. Both were seen walking alone along roads leading away from their safety zones, but more importantly, both were seen hitchhiking during the hours or minutes before their disappearances.

These two girls were trusting people. Paula was fearless about hitchhiking, had done so in the past, and obtained at least one ride toward Woodford Hollow from someone she didn't know. Connie was described as not being afraid of strangers. Her father once said, "She was brought up that way on the ranch. She would talk to anyone."[155] This was evidenced by the fact that she stopped twice to ask complete strangers for directions on the roads leading to Lakeville center.

If someone wanted to drive from the center of Lakeville, Connecticut to the center of Bennington, Vermont, they would likely take Route 44 west to Route 22 north in New York State. On the surface, driving Route 44 directly to Route 22 seems to be a sensible route and most people would take it to travel into New York – going directly through the center of the village of Millerton. But drivers intimately familiar with the area who wanted to head north would opt for a more direct, less known alternative. They would head west on Route 44 but would then take a right onto Belgo Road (the intersection where Connie Smith was last seen). They would then proceed a little over two miles where Belgo Road becomes Shagroy Road once it crosses the New York border. They would then take a right onto Rudd Pond Road taking the driver to Route 22.

This north-south artery heads straight up along New York's eastern border and runs roughly parallel with the Connecticut, Massachusetts and Vermont state lines. From its beginning in Bronx, New York, to its northern terminus at the Canadian border, Route 22 is 361 miles long and is the third longest highway in New York. Route 22 is primarily separated from the three states to the east by the Taconic Range of mountains. It passes the length of the western Connecticut border, along a portion of Taconic State Park and Bash Bish Falls State Park. It then meanders through the

Lebanon Valley to Lebanon Springs where mineral springs once rejuvenated weary travelers, and continues along the Taconic Range that extends along the southwestern Vermont border. Once near Vermont, one simply connects briefly to Route 7 and then to Route 9 that leads directly into Bennington center. A few miles down this road to the east is Woodford Hollow, where Paula Welden sought the Long Trail entrance.

Route 22 was (and still is) a convenient, direct route and provides easy access to the three bordering New England states. Before the modern interstate highway system was built, this route was frequently used by motorists and truckers. It offered easy access to Connecticut, Massachusetts and Vermont and connected with other major arteries to Albany, Syracuse and points west. One favorite route for leaf-peepers recommended by the Automobile Club of Hartford was to drive through northwestern Connecticut, through western Massachusetts to Bennington, Vermont. The recommended return trip was via Route 22 on the other side of the Taconic Range passing through Lebanon Springs and crossing over the border to Stockbridge, Massachusetts, and continuing south through Lakeville, Connecticut, before returning to Hartford.[156]

In the search for cases similar to the Welden/Smith disappearances, it was easy to become sidetracked with the baffling Long Trail vanishings and high-profile unsolved murders with different circumstances. But there was one missing person case, considerably lower in profile, that was eventually considered solved and thus did not appear on any police department's "cold case" list. Though there were several local news articles about this disappearance it didn't attain the almost supernatural aura that would enshroud the disappearances in the Green Mountains. At the time, it appeared to be an isolated case. Yet looking back on this case, it had many of the same elements as the later Paula Welden and Connie Smith cases.

Michael C. Dooling

Lebanon Valley
Undated Postcard

Along New York's Route 22, about a 40-mile drive south of Bennington and a 46-mile drive north of Lakeville, is the small town of New Lebanon in Columbia County, New York. This community has historic significance for several reasons. In the 19th century, the surrounding area had a significant community of Shakers. By 1936, their numbers had dwindled and the sect had nearly died off. With fewer converts as time went on and the fact that they strictly abided by celibacy pretty much determined the eventual fate of the self-sufficient communal group.

Completely opposite to the austere lifestyle of the Shakers in New Lebanon, the nearby village of Lebanon Springs attracted the rich and famous as a vacation destination. The main attractions were its mineral springs; those who bathed in them claimed they were relieved of many types of ills. The Lebanon Springs were renowned far and wide, and over the years the guests who visited there were among the nation's elite. Daniel Webster and the Marquis de Lafayette were guests there, as were the Lowells from Boston, the

Van Rensselaers and the Van Burens from New York. Cottages, guest houses and spacious hotels had sprung up around the springs, and the largest of them, Columbia Hall, closed about 1900. A traveler's handbook from the 19th century provides a charming description of the springs:

> This justly celebrated Spa is delightfully situated near the division line between the States of New York and Massachusetts, 25 miles from Albany. There are fine accommodations at the Springs, which are situated on the side of a hill, overlooking one of the most lovely valleys of our country. The cavity from which the water gushes is 10 feet in diameter, and the quantity is sufficient to drive a mill. Its temperature is uniformly 72°. It is tasteless, inodorous, and soft, admirably adapted to bathing, and excellent in cutaneous affections, rheumatism, internal obstructions, liver complaint, nervous debility, etc.[157]

Much of the tourist trade to Lebanon Springs diminished after the closing of Columbia Hall, but cottages, guest houses and private homes still drew smaller numbers of visitors. Although the summer visitors swelled the ranks in the town, New Lebanon barely had 1,200 people living there year 'round in the 1930s.

It was a cool spring day, the second day of April 1936, and Minnie (Wilhelmina) McGonagle had overnight guests at her home – her son Harry Hull and his 22-year-old[158] daughter Katherine. Minnie lived by herself on Spring Hill Road just a few hundred yards from the famous springs and just below the former site of Columbia Hall. The Hull family was well entrenched in Lebanon Springs. Three generations of Hull men ran Columbia Hall for much of the 19th century and one of them, Henry, had married Minnie. They had several children and, after Henry died, Minnie married

James McGonagle and she again became a widow in 1931. The members of the Hull family were frequent visitors to the "Springs" area, drawn there by Minnie and the bucolic surroundings of the region.

Columbia Hall is the Large Building in the Distance
Minnie McGonagle's house is obscured by trees.
Early Postcard Image

Minnie McGonagle's son Harry was a civil engineer, working as Village Engineer and living in Saranac Lake, New York, where he was one of the town's prominent citizens. Harry, his wife Florence and their two daughters, Katherine and her older sister Marjorie, lived at Saranac Lake. The girls attended the village school and both were later trained as stenographers. About 1926, Harry and Florence Hull apparently separated. With her children and her mother Lillian, Florence lived at 743 Lancaster Avenue in Syracuse. Marjorie was employed there and remained behind that April.

When Katherine arrived in Lebanon Springs, she intended to spend that entire summer with her grandmother. What started out as a pleasant family visit soon turned into heartbreak. Harry and Katherine arrived that morning and had lunch with Minnie. After lunch, Harry began to unload Katherine's suitcases, leather bags and boxes from his car. Katherine, apparently anxious to start her vacation, decided to take a walk. Around noon, she happily waved goodbye to her father and walked up the hill toward the warm mineral springs. A short way up the hill, Spring Hill Road meets Pool Hill Road and together they form an inverted "U" with both roads leading downhill to Main Street. Pool Hill Road intersects Main Street near the old Lebanon Springs Road that traverses the mountains separating New York from Massachusetts. From Main Street, that dirt road (now more trail than road), rises more than 800 feet as it winds over the next two miles and leads into Pittsfield State Forest in Hancock and eventually to Pittsfield, Massachusetts.

According to her father, Katherine was "light-hearted" as she walked toward the springs and had told him she would be back in time for supper. When she left her grandmother's house, she was wearing a blue dress, sports sweater of a grey mixture, black low shoes with rubber overshoes, dark stockings, green coat with a fur collar and a brown tam-o-shanter. She carried a brown handbag but took no extra clothing, luggage, money, food or any other personal belongings. Katherine's father watched his happy-go-lucky daughter walk out of sight that afternoon not knowing it was the last time he would see her.

As darkness fell and Katherine didn't return to her grandmother's house, her father became worried and telephoned the New York State Police to report her missing. The people of sleepy Lebanon Springs rarely experienced police matters of any significance and when the New York State Police at the sub-station in New Lebanon received a call from a worried father regarding his missing daughter, it was taken in appropriate stride. After all, she had probably simply gotten lost or run away from home and the matter would be resolved rather quickly.

The last person who went missing that caused a local stir

disappeared forty-nine years earlier. In 1887, Miss E. Carrie Sweet, age 17, from Stephentown, New York, had ostensibly traveled by train from Troy to Lebanon Springs to take painting lessons. When she didn't return home, searches were conducted at both ends of the train line. Some believed she might have joined a convent, having once expressed interest in becoming a nun, and her father personally contacted every convent in the area but didn't find her.[159] The next speculation was that she might have gone to Europe to join a convent. Carrie's father visited New York City and sought the help of the Pinkerton Agency to follow up this possibility with foreign contacts, apparently with no luck. Her family, friends and the investigators were completely stumped. Then, twenty-eight days after she disappeared, she returned home. She had gone to Europe and hadn't told her parents because she thought they would have stopped her.[160]

But Katherine Hull's case was different. She hadn't been on a train, didn't have any extra clothing, nor any money to speak of. A search of the surrounding area was begun. Family, neighbors and friends joined the state police in an organized search. The Boy Scouts were called out of school on Thursday by their scoutmaster, Gordon Turner, to assist with the search that continued through the weekend. Mrs. Hull was notified in Syracuse and impatiently waited there in case Katherine headed home. Shoe prints that could have been Katherine's were found in the soft dirt along the road but eventually disappeared. The search yielded no clues as to her whereabouts and Katherine never showed up at her grandmother's home. The state police were convinced Katherine was no longer in the nearby Berkshire foothills and called off the search. On Monday April 6th, the scouts stopped searching and returned to school. Nonetheless, on Monday, Katherine's father continued searching by himself.

CLUELESS IN NEW ENGLAND

The New York State Police investigators, Corporal T. R. Ford assisted by Trooper Lyle Closson, interviewed people in the area hoping someone had seen Katherine after she left her grandmother's house. A high school student, Marion L. Cameron of West Lebanon, told police she had seen a woman matching Katherine's description getting into an automobile with a man and a woman on Thursday afternoon. The car drove away in the westbound direction toward Albany. Since there was nothing remarkable about the event, she didn't make any particular note of the make and model of the car nor its license number. Based on this sighting, the state police became convinced Katherine had gone off with friends or had headed back to Syracuse.

Two other witnesses claimed they saw Katherine that day.[161] Bernie Richmond of New Lebanon Center owned a general store in a building that also housed the local post office at the intersection of Route 20 and Mill Road. Richmond's store faced Route 20 and from that vantage point he saw Katherine walk by his windows. Supporting Marion Cameron's statement, another witness believed he saw her enter a car. Maurice Potter of New Lebanon reportedly saw a woman of her description entering someone's automobile but the exact location of the sighting, as with Marion Cameron's sighting, is unknown. Another news report mentioned an unnamed driver who actually picked her up and gave her a ride. "Motorists reported having seen the young woman walking on the highway near Lebanon Springs while one told authorities that he gave a young woman, answering the description of Miss Hull, a ride toward Albany."[162] A newspaper article from 1944 reinforced that report, "A salesman driving in that section (Lebanon Springs) is said to have identified pictures of Miss Hull as being those of a girl to whom he gave a ride...the trail dropped there."[163]

More than a week after Katherine went missing, New York State Police Sergeant H. A. Keator told reporters, "Not a single clue to the young woman's whereabouts had developed in the nine days since she was seen climbing into an automobile."[164] All her known friends were contacted, all places she might have gone were checked, and circulars were sent out. A worried Harry Hull visited the state police barracks daily for updates but learned nothing to alleviate his fears.

Mrs. McGonagle described Katherine as "serious minded, of religious leanings, and never has been interested in the companionship of men."[165] At one point in the investigation, Katherine's parents expressed the possibility that she, like Carrie Sweet nearly fifty years earlier, might have left to enter a convent. Police immediately contacted convents in the area in hopes one had taken her in, but the effort only elicited prayers for her safe return. Area hotels were also checked, to no avail. From all appearances and given past jaunts, Katherine would have told someone if she intended to leave for an overnight and she would have packed some clothes for the trip. Like Paula Welden and Connie Smith in later years, she had done neither.

More than two weeks after Katherine was last seen, with no other clues to go on, state police investigators started to discount the witnesses who had seen her hitchhiking. That being said, it was reported that Katherine's grandmother told the police she frequently hitchhiked:

> (Katherine) was fond of walking and frequently had gone on hitchhiking jaunts before. On previous occasions, however, she always left a note or sent a postcard. This time no note was found and no communication had been received...It had been Miss Hull's habit to stay at the Y.W.C.A. while traveling, but a check on the Albany and Troy Y.W.C.A.'s established she had not stopped there Thursday or Friday night.[166]

More than two weeks after her daughter went missing, Mrs. Hull received a telephone call at home from a woman who claimed she had a tip as to Katherine's whereabouts. The woman called her on April 19th and, according to one newspaper article,[167] told Mrs. Hull she would "come forward and tell all she knows" if she could be granted immunity from prosecution in case she could be implicated in a criminal act. The article continued:

> "The woman," Mrs. Hull said, "wasted no words." She told Mrs. Hull that, if she wished to learn something to her "advantage" she should seek her missing daughter in Utica. And she asked Mrs. Hull if Katherine knew any "girls in Utica." Mrs. Hull said, "Not that I know of." "Well," said the voice over the telephone, "I would advise you to investigate these two addresses in Utica." She then gave what purported to be two street numbers. One was in the 800 block of a street which turned out to be only six blocks long and the other was the home of a quiet elderly couple...The woman refused to say anything about herself when Mrs. Hull asked who she was. "I don't want to get mixed up in this," she said.

Mrs. Hull later remembered her daughter had gone to Utica seeking a stenographer position several months earlier and thought there might be a connection. This portion of the investigation was conducted by Syracuse District Attorney William Martin and Assistant District Attorney Donald Mawhinney, assisted by Sheriff Howard Mosher. They believed the call may have had some importance and the Utica tip was thoroughly investigated. No connection to Katherine Hull could be established.

More than a month after the disappearance, another search party was formed. On May 5th, Sheriff Milton Saulpaugh formed a posse of Civilian Conservation Corps campers to search the dense woods near Katherine's grandmother's home. This search had more of a somber tone to it than the earlier ones. The search party was working on the assumption that Katherine may have gotten lost and died of exposure in the woods. Their efforts failed to reveal any new information.

After one month passed, investigators decided to put up posters of the missing girl in railroad depots and bus terminals around the state of New York. Katherine was described as 5'6" tall, weighing 135 pounds, with bobbed brown hair, light complexion, hazel eyes, and a scar beneath her right ear. The poster also indicated that she might be suffering from amnesia.

> Characteristics:
>
> Very quiet, seldom smiles, concentrates deeply, religious, cannot be drawn out in conversation, not apt to talk about herself or confide in anyone, very polite and well-mannered, quite attractive but sober-faced, very neat in her dress and appearance. Any peculiar traits are not objectionable and is a girl who could not be disliked. If seen on the street she walks quite fast with peculiar striding up and down motion. Walks with eyes straight ahead, as if sighting something in the distance and hurrying to get there.
>
> Employers take notice: A good typist, takes dictation quite rapidly, very neat in her work and a steady hard worker; when spoken to by friends or employer is not apt to change expression, either by flicker of eyelash or movement of lips – a regular poker face. Likes children and might be found working in private family in rural districts of eastern or central New York. All city hospitals, institutions, employment agencies, churches, etc. take notice of any girl with lost or hazy memory. Last attended Episcopal church in Syracuse, N.Y.[168]

As word spread about the missing girl, calls started to come in with sightings. A waitress and diner owner in North Tarrytown,

Clueless in New England

New York believed one of their customers was Katherine. A gentleman from Queens sent a photograph of a girl who was rooming with his mother that he thought might have been Katherine. Police showed the photograph to Mrs. Hull, but it was not her daughter. In August, an employee at Remington Rand Corporation noticed a woman by the name of "Catherine" Hull had applied for a job there, and called the police. They learned she was staying at the Yates Hotel in Syracuse and, with Mrs. Hull accompanying them, police staked out the lobby for eighty minutes waiting for her to return. When she walked into the lobby, it took Mrs. Hull only a moment to determine the applicant wasn't her Katherine.

It wasn't until four months passed that a reward was finally offered in the Hull case. In August, Florence Hull offered a $1,000 reward for information leading to the location of her daughter. The effort was in vain and no new leads developed. Mrs. Hull also announced her hope that "G-men" would assist in the search but there is no evidence that federal agents became involved in the case.

Questions whether Katherine ran away with friends, got lost in the woods and died of exposure, joined a convent, or something more sinister lingered in the minds of her parents, her sister Marjorie and her grandmother. The family became convinced that Katherine had developed amnesia and was wandering around a nearby city. This was a purely optimistic belief on their part; there was no evidence whatsoever to support it. Years went by with not one clue surfacing as to what had happened to Katherine Hull. Undoubtedly, the family was haunted by the memory of Katherine and how she could have disappeared without a trace. That is, until December 1943.

Michael C. Dooling

Reward Poster
Courtesy of The Berkshire Eagle

Clueless in New England

On Wednesday, December 8th, a hunting party including Harold D. Boland and Raymond L. Scace, neighbors living on West Street in Pittsfield, Mass., were tracking deer on the western slope of West Mountain. Boland noticed numerous deer tracks below the ridge of West Mountain and positioned himself hoping deer would cross his path. Alone at this point, he turned his head and suddenly noticed a human skull staring him in the face; it was bizarrely propped in the crotch of tree. Boland's story was quoted in the newspaper:[169]

> I was so startled that for a few minutes I stood petrified. Then when my friends came up I showed them the skull and we all wondered how it ever got there. Poking 'round in the snow under the hemlock I found what looked like a human leg bone. With me at the time were Charles Parker, William Cody, George, Raymond, Ralph, Frederick and James Scace. It was late in the afternoon as we started home, all deerless. I was carrying the skull and the leg bone when we met Raymond Marcel, a Pittsfield policeman. I showed Marcel what I had found and from the nearest house he telephoned to Detective Horgan and the state police.

James Scace was Raymond's son and remembers that day well. He was fifteen at the time and it was his first hunting expedition. That week was always reserved by his father, friends and family for deer hunting and the group entered the mountains from West Street in Pittsfield walking on Lebanon Springs Road. There were certain landmarks they always used as reference points, one being the aircraft beacon that towered over the top of West Mountain. Another was a line of telephone cables, connecting Boston with Albany, that traversed the mountain. His father had helped construct them years before and a right-of-way connected them. As the younger Scace hiked toward the hemlock with the rest of the party, he remembers Boland walking toward them brandishing the skull in his hand saying, "Look what I found." The entire party was shocked by the find and James admitted he was a bit scared. It was the kind of event one doesn't forget, even sixty-four years later.[170]

Despite a biting sub-zero wind blowing from the west, a search party was formed to look for more evidence. The group consisted of Lieutenant Detective John F. Horgan of the Pittsfield Barracks, who headed up the investigation, State Patrolman Edward F. Nolan, and Massachusetts State Police photographer Wilfred Sirois. With Mr. Boland as their guide, the party hiked more than three miles over the snow-covered dirt road and trails to the hemlock tree below the ridge of West Mountain and searched the area using rakes and shovels. According to one news account,[171] "The bones were all found on the surface of the earth or slightly covered by debris, precluding the possibility that the body had been covered in a shallow grave." They found most of the skeleton including the lower jaw with most of the teeth intact, part of the spine, several ribs, clavicle, arm and leg bones. By the end of the search, the skeleton was lacking only a few vertebrae and part of the pelvis.

At this point in time, the exact location where the skeleton was found is uncertain. The remains were found just over the state border in Hancock, Massachusetts, on West Mountain. Police records, that certainly would have contained detailed information, are long gone. Newspaper accounts varied from one article to another and used different points as references. Depending on the account, the skeleton was found "a little more than a mile up the mountain from" or "in the immediate vicinity of" Lebanon Springs; "less than four miles from" or "near" Minnie McGonagle's home. According to one account,[172] the remains were located "three miles from the so-called Wager farm, which in turn is a mile from Lebanon Springs." Attempts to identify the location of the Wager farm have been unsuccessful. No one interviewed on either side of the mountain recalls a farm with that name. One farm was located at

914 West Street in Pittsfield at which a gardener named Alfred Wagar lived for a short time in the 1920s. That could be the farm referred to but, according to two members of the Scace family who lived in the West Street vicinity at the time, there was no farm in that area with that nickname.

Fortunately, James Scace has a respectable recollection of events of that memorable day. Using the aircraft beacon as a reference point, combined with his remembrance of the location of the old telephone lines, he indicated the approximate location of the skeletal remains on an old topographical map. According to his examination of the map and his recollections, the remains were found about a quarter of a mile northwest of the old beacon about halfway between the top of West Mountain and Lebanon Springs Road.

In 1936, West Street connected to (and still does connect to) Lebanon Springs Road, the packed dirt road that leads over the mountain. According to news accounts, the state police entered the mountain area from West Street and hiked 3½ miles to the site where the skeleton was found. At another time of the year, they would have been able to drive in much of the way but the road wasn't plowed during the winter months. James Scace remembers the skeleton was found off the right-of-way near the telephone cables on the west side of West Mountain. He also recalls numerous trails they had followed up the mountain leading to the site. Scace recollects, "...the skull was found due north of the telephone line on an old trail – either a deer trail or more probably one left by CCC activities in the late '30s; they covered most of the mountains."[173]

It didn't take long for investigators to consider a possible connection between the remains discovered on West Mountain and the disappearance of Katherine Hull more than seven years earlier. The remains were sent to the Massachusetts State Police Crime Lab in Boston to be further examined by chemists and medical experts with hopes of obtaining clues to identify them.

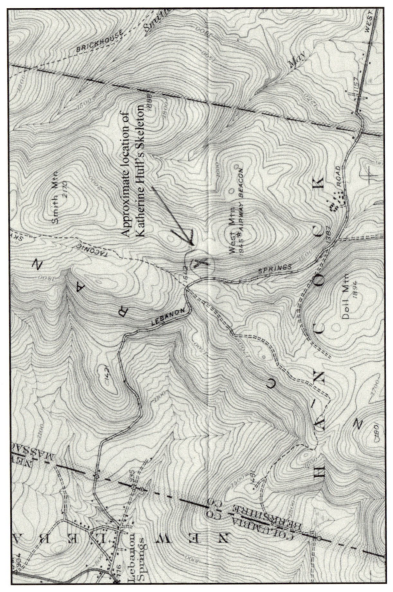

**James Scace's Remembrance of the Location
of Katherine Hull's Skeleton**
USGS Map, Pittsfield West (Mass.) Quadrangle, 1947

CLUELESS IN NEW ENGLAND

Dr. Alan R. Moritz, Massachusetts State Pathologist, examined the remains to determine the approximate age, gender, and height of the individual. Moritz was quite renowned in his field and was professor of legal medicine at Harvard University. Dr. Albert England, the district medical examiner, examined the skull and noted the upper jaw protruded over the lower jaw, a number of teeth in the lower jaw had fillings, and one tooth was set slightly behind the one immediately in front of it. He concluded these factors would be of great assistance in determining the identity of the individual.

Investigators Discussing Katherine's Skull
(Left to Right: Howard Mosher of the District Attorney's Office, Sgt. William Stevenson of the New York State Police, Sheriff Robert Wasmer holding skull, Lt. John Horgan of the Massachusetts State Police)
Courtesy of the Onondaga Historical Association

There was considerable controversy over whether the bones could be those of Katherine Hull. Using a standard formula for calculating a person's height from the length of the thigh bone it appeared the skeleton could not be Katherine's. The calculation, known as the Krogman formula, determined that an individual's height was 1.88 times the length of the thigh bone plus a constant of 813.06 mm (about 32 inches). The thigh bone was $17\frac{1}{2}"$ long which would make the height of the person about $5'5\frac{1}{2}"$. Katherine had been described as being 5'6". Later it was determined she was slightly shorter than the height measurement originally printed on missing person circulars, thereby accounting for the discrepancy.

On the afternoon of December 11th, Corporal Louis Perachi of the Pittsfield barracks delivered a clue found among the skeletal remains to the state police laboratory. It was described in the log book of laboratory submissions as a "Small piece of cloth found near human skeleton on West Mount. in town Hancock by Lt. Jh. F. Horgan,"[174] and was assigned Lab Number 2059. Scientific examination was performed on the color and weave of the cloth remnant and provided evidence that it may have been from the green coat Katherine wore the afternoon she disappeared. Lieutenant Joseph T. Walker, state police chemist, performed the analysis and wrote a report that he sent by teletype back to Pittsfield investigators. The original report doesn't exist anymore but the results were reported in the newspaper. Walker concluded[175]:

> The fragment of cloth found on West Mountain is of wool loosely woven medium fabric with novelty design similar to what would be incorporated in a woman's suit, wool skirt or lightweight coat. The color at present is light brown, but this could easily have been green or khaki originally. There is some suggestion of green at present.

CLUELESS IN NEW ENGLAND

Massachusetts authorities sought assistance from the New York State Police to help identify the remains. Inspector Edward Hageman located a dentist who had worked on Katherine's teeth in hopes he could identify them. Unfortunately, he had only cleaned her teeth. A dentist from Auburn, New York was identified who had acquired the practice of a dentist who had filled cavities in Katherine's teeth in May 1928. Dr. G. Burnett Atwater reviewed the records from his father-in-law, Dr. Herman L. Ketchum, who had put silver fillings in her upper right wisdom tooth and upper right molar. He also had put a gold filling in her upper right lateral tooth. The skull contained that tooth but it contained a silver filling. Dr. Atwater removed some of the silver filling and found part of a gold filling underneath. Apparently the skull's owner had more problems with the same tooth and another dentist had filled it with silver.

The perplexing question as to why the skull was found in the crotch of a tree was finally answered. Another deer hunter, Francis G. Van Slyck of Massachusetts Avenue in Pittsfield, had been hunting in the area two days before his nephew, Harold Boland, found the skull. He was hunting on the side of West Mountain and noticed a skull under the large hemlock. It was embedded in the snow and he irreverently kicked it to dislodge it. Van Slyck positioned it in the crotch of a nearby tree, intending to pick it up on his way back from hunting that day and to bring it back to town. He followed deer tracks to another part of the forest and returned home by a different route. The hunter left the skull sitting in the tree without returning to the site and, for reasons unknown, without notifying any authorities.

The Massachusetts and New York state police started to track down Katherine's relatives. Her grandmother had moved to Florida and her mother was reportedly living in Miami. When Mrs. Hull heard the investigation was again active it served to re-open old wounds and she was understandably distraught. Katherine's sister

Marjorie still lived in Syracuse and Harry Hull shared his time between Saranac Lake and Daytona Beach. He was in a state of denial that the skull was Katherine's, choosing to believe she was still alive and "may have joined an order of Episcopal nuns, a wish that she had expressed on many occasions."[176] Unbelieving, he left for his Florida home before the remains were positively identified.

Given the evidence gained from the pathologist's examination, dental records and chemical analysis, state police concluded the remains found on West Mountain were those of Katherine Hull. The case was closed once her remains were identified and there was no investigation into possible foul play. Because Katherine's disappearance wasn't considered a capital crime or a high profile case, almost no records exist today. In the eyes of investigators the case had been "solved" once the victim was identified. The New York and Massachusetts state police departments have no records relating to any aspect of the case other than a single logbook entry relating to the fabric of her coat. Like all large organizations, the state police periodically purge files that are no longer considered necessary to keep. It appears Katherine Hull's disappearance was one of those cases that lacked sufficient importance and interest to warrant storing the files.

Attempts to obtain autopsy results also failed to locate any records. The Massachusetts Chief Medical Examiner's Office, established in 1983, is responsible for maintaining autopsy records. Prior to 1983, pathologists performed autopsies and turned in their summary reports to law enforcement but the actual autopsy records were maintained by the individual doctors. The medical examiner's office attempted to retrieve older autopsy records with limited success. Attempts to track down the records of the pathologist who performed the examination, Dr. Alan Moritz, resulted in failure as well. There were no newspaper accounts regarding the postmortem examination of the skeletal remains that indicated Katherine may have been murdered, or that she had not been murdered, nor that she had fallen and broken any bones. Evidence of Katherine dying of exposure, being sexually assaulted or having been strangled was long before destroyed by decomposition and the forces of nature. Even though the police had her remains in their possession, they still had no clues as to what had happened to Katherine Hull.

The State of Massachusetts released Katherine's remains and on October 5, 1944, they were cremated at the Mount Auburn Cemetery. Her ashes were interred at the Cemetery of the Evergreens in New Lebanon just a few miles from the location where her remains had been found. An entry in the cemetery records that documented her burial indicates simply, "unknown cause of death." Strangely, attempts to locate Katherine's death certificate have led to dead ends. The death certificate should have been filed in the town where the death occurred. The town clerk in Hancock was unable to locate the certificate or any record that it had been filed and was at a loss to say where it could have been filed. Similar efforts in Pittsfield and a search of the statewide records stored in Dorchester, revealed nothing. Searches of records in Columbia and Onondaga Counties in New York found no indication the death certificate exists. Her death certificate does not appear to have been properly filed.

Detective Horgan was of the opinion that Katherine suffered from periodic episodes of amnesia. He believed she walked up the mountain road for more than a mile and at some point went off into the woods toward the ridge of West Mountain. Horgan speculated she must have had one of her amnesia spells and became lost, dying of exposure under the hemlock. The weather conditions supported this possibility. The Pittsfield City Hall weather report for the day Katherine disappeared finds the minimum temperature in town was thirty degrees with a half inch of snow and .65 inches of rain. It appears the precipitation occurred later that day and on West

Mountain may have been more in the form of snow.

The died-of-exposure theory of Katherine's demise ignores the investigation conducted by the New York State Police nearly eight years earlier in which several witnesses claimed they saw a woman resembling Katherine walking by Richmond's store or hitchhiking and getting into someone's car. Although Horgan's theory could be correct, it ignored important evidence and was purely speculative. It was a convenient and simplistic explanation of the basic facts – woman goes for a walk, woman disappears, and woman's skeleton is found in the woods years later. It was an expedient way to close a case there was little hope of solving.

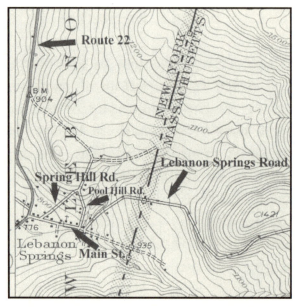

Area Where Katherine Hull Went Walking
USGS Map, Pittsfield West (Mass.) Quadrangle, 1947

Taking the New York State Police investigation into account, the story is more complex. Katherine Hull left her grandmother's house on Spring Hill Road and walked uphill for a few hundred feet. Near the top, she had two options. She could have gone right and walked downhill on Pool Hill Road toward Main Street. Or, she could have taken a left and followed a dirt road for more than a half-mile down to Route 22. Had she taken the first route to Main Street (that also connects to Route 22), Katherine may have considered taking a left and heading uphill on Lebanon Springs Road – which promised to be a fairly steep and tiring walk. Katherine appears to have decided to explore the Lebanon Valley itself and either walked or thumbed the short distance to Route 22 and took a left in a southerly direction toward the center of New Lebanon. Although she may have walked the $3^1/_2$ miles to Richmond's Store located on the Columbia Pike (Route 20), she likely hitchhiked and may have obtained a ride with the salesman who claimed to have picked her up.

Where Katherine's destination might have been is unclear. Route 20 heads west toward Albany and perhaps Katherine thought the state capital might be a good destination for an afternoon's adventure. After all, it was only about thirty miles away and an easy ride. There was a considerable amount of farmland between New Lebanon and Albany, and not many tourist destinations in that direction. Regardless of what she was planning, Katherine was observed hitchhiking and climbing into someone's car heading in a westerly direction. Then something happened. Perhaps someone to whom she entrusted her safety while hitchhiking didn't fulfill that trust. Instead of taking Katherine to her destination of choice, the individual(s) may have abducted, assaulted and murdered her.

The supposed assault and murder could have happened on the slope of West Mountain where she may have been forcibly taken. Or, the crimes may have been carried out elsewhere with her body driven up Lebanon Springs Road, carried or driven up the hillside using the right-of-way to the telephone poles or one of the trails known by local hunters, and then dumped under the hemlock tree. Lonely Lebanon Springs Road sneaks along the base of West

Mountain. The ridge of West Mountain is about one-quarter-mile uphill from the dirt road and James Scace estimated that Katherine's skeleton was found about half that distance up the slope. Two things are certain. Whoever might have carried out these violations to Katherine would have been familiar with the mountain roads and trails between Route 22 and Pittsfield, and that person attempted to hide the body in such a secluded spot that it would not easily be found. Perhaps the perpetrator was more successful with future abductions of young women and in hiding their bodies.

Katherine Hull's Footstone

Chapter V

"Where have all the young girls gone?
Long time passing
Where have all the young girls gone?
Long time ago"

Pete Seeger, *Where Have All the Flowers Gone?*

CLUELESS IN NEW ENGLAND

The Hunting Ground

As the decades of the twentieth century rolled by, law enforcement agencies began to lose their naiveté and became considerably more sophisticated in how they viewed different types of crimes and the criminals who committed them. Criminal investigation became more organized and rooted in science. Lone and untrained sheriffs organizing posses to search for missing persons were replaced with trained, professional police departments. The psychological and jurisdictional barriers presented by state lines were replaced with increased cooperation between agencies. Examination of physical evidence became vastly more scientific and DNA analysis took hold as an invaluable identification tool. Postmortem examinations became more standardized and sophisticated. And the field of criminology and psychological profiling, in its early infancy during the 1950s, developed significantly and now provide a better understanding of the behaviors and motives exhibited by different types of criminals.

Gradually, law enforcement agencies realized that sex offenses were rampant and sex offenders needed to be reined in. FBI Director J. Edgar Hoover wrote[177] that in 1953 sex offenses had reached an all-time high and "the degenerate sex offender looms today as a menace to the safety and well-being of every boy and girl in America." He went on to say that punishment didn't reform sex offenders and that most such criminals were repeat offenders. Hoover criticized the court system for treating "mad degenerates" as minor offenders and releasing them "when they have no more right to be at liberty than mad dogs have." Although Hoover suggested psychiatric and medical treatment for sex offenders, he also realized that such treatment was not always successful and he believed the offenders should be banished from society through long term institutionalization.

The State of Connecticut attempted to thwart the ability of sex offenders to operate over a large area. A law was passed in 1955 that suspended their drivers' licenses if they used a motor vehicle in the execution of their crimes. The law was relatively ineffectual. Communication among the police, the courts, and the Motor Vehicle Department was poor. Information wasn't shared and a license was revoked only if a specific request was made to do so. Convictions for crimes prior to 1955 were excluded from the law allowing George J. Davies, who had been convicted and jailed for molesting two young girls before the law went into effect, to keep his license. He later used his vehicle when committing the murders of Gaetane Boivin and Brenda Doucette, and probably would still have done so even if he didn't have a license to drive. The law was difficult to enforce; a determined sex offender wouldn't think twice about driving with a suspended license.

A few years later, police attained a better understanding of sex offenders and of serial killers, whose crimes often involve sexual offenses as well. The ability of police to act quickly, coordinate activities between agencies, and better analyze information has been vastly improved through advancements in police procedures, centralized criminal records, and the accessibility of fingerprint files to all police departments. Psychological profiling, studies of the geographic patterns of serial criminals, sex offender databases and the Amber Alert system for abducted children have been useful in solving serial crimes and locating missing persons. Such wasn't the case when police were investigating the Hull – Welden – Smith cases. Yet, some of the tools used by modern law enforcement agencies may be useful in looking back on the three disappearances.

Was it possible that Katherine Hull was the first (or at least one of the earliest) in a series of abductions and murders of young women near the western border of New England? Although rather arbitrarily explained away as a lost-in-the-woods case, Katherine Hull's disappearance has many of the same elements of the later cases. Importantly, unlike the disappearances of Paula Welden and Connie Smith, Katherine's skeletal remains were found. The marked similarities of the circumstances surrounding the three disappearances, the proximity of the cases to the New York border, and the fact that the bodies of the three young women were intentionally hidden so they wouldn't be found, all point to the possibility they could be related to one another. Might a serial murderer been active along the New York border, preying on young women hitchhiking alone along country roads?

The distances between the incidents, the time lapse between events, the involvement of three separate state police departments, Vermont's rudimentary sheriff system, and mis-categorizing the Katherine Hull case after her remains were found all contributed to "linkage blindness." The three cases were never connected to one another and no similarities among them were ever examined by investigators. There is nothing in the Paula Welden state police files nor in newspaper accounts that made any reference to Katherine Hull's disappearance; nor were there any references in the Connie Smith state police files to the Paula Welden or Katherine Hull cases.

One of the more significant similarities among the cases is the fact that all three were seen hitchhiking shortly before they disappeared. A large study[178] of the types of people that serial killers prey upon found the most frequent victims are either female college students or prostitutes, followed by young boys or girls, and the third most frequent targets are hitchhikers. Katherine had only one of those characteristics working against her – being a hitchhiker. Paula and Connie each fell into two categories: Paula - a hitchhiking college student, and Connie - a young girl who was hitchhiking.

At first glance, Connie Smith seemed too young to be part of a possible series of murders including 18-year-old Paula Welden and 22- year-old Katherine Hull. But given the fact that she looked older, and knowing that other serial killers have selected victims in a similar age range, it is in the realm of possibility that the three could have been abducted by the same individual.

Today, we discourage hitchhiking as a potentially dangerous activity for both the hitchhiker and the driver but it has not always been that way. Putting out one's thumb had become a common method of traveling during the Great Depression years as all sorts of people sought work and had little money, much less their own automobile. As a matter of fact, hitchhiking was given tacit acceptance by the federal government during those years when the Federal Transient Bureau dealt with the large number of unemployed persons who were migrating to other areas of the country to find employment. Transients were promised a room and a hot meal at camps set up by the bureau around the country as long as they could get to them. The bureau operated such camps until it closed its doors in 1936. During those years, thumbing rides around the country was an accepted fact of life.

Problems arose as a result of random hitchhikers obtaining rides from random drivers. Warnings of the potential dangers of picking up hitchhikers were publicized to drivers. Some of them would rob the driver who picked them up, and in some cases murder them. Other warnings were publicized to the hitchhikers themselves and alerted them to the same types of crimes being carried out by drivers. By 1937, fourteen states had passed laws giving a "thumbs down" to hitchhiking and more than half the states had done so by 1950. Nonetheless, hitchhiking was part of the American psyche and many people continued to stick out their thumbs even in states where the practice had been outlawed.

Our presumed killer may have encountered many hitchhikers

along his driving route and whether he would pick up the person or not depended on opportunity, gender and age of the hitchhiker, the degree of seclusion where he encountered the individual, presence of others in the area, proximity to a populated area, access to good escape routes, etc. He may well have picked up many more hitchhikers than he actually assaulted. Perhaps there were some physical characteristics or behaviors of the potential victims that compelled him to carry out his mission or to abort it. It would not be surprising if he pleasantly and safely gave rides to some young women, who never suspected the driver was dangerous nor ever knew how close they had come to their demise. Nor would it be surprising if he had attempted to (or actually did) assault some of them, and they managed to escape his grasp.

Unfortunately, "almost crimes" and non-capital crimes usually don't make it into a police department's cold case files. If such records do exist there could be a wealth of information in those files about women who had possibly seen and interacted with the murderer. The act of hitchhiking placed Katherine, Paula and Connie squarely in a potential danger zone. Each was alone, far from people and places they knew well, and had limited escape options at their disposal. They innocently and unwittingly put themselves at risk and at the mercy or impulse of whoever happened by and picked them up.

One famous serial killer primarily murdered hitchhikers in the early 1970s. Edmund Kemper, who killed his grandparents as a teenager and five years later was released from a state hospital, started preying on female hitchhikers. Over the course of a year, he murdered six young women ranging in age from 15 to 23 and became known as the "Coed Killer." Before he started murdering the girls he picked up, Kemper had given rides to many female hitchhikers and developed some skills at making the girls feel comfortable about entering his vehicle. If a girl seemed hesitant to get into his car, he used a very simple gesture that communicated to them that he wasn't particularly interested in anything other than offering them a ride. He would purposely glance at his watch to subtly communicate to them he was a busy man and had an appointment. The girls were reassured by this little action – that their ride would be strictly business and Kemper had to be someplace at a certain time – and they voluntarily climbed into his vehicle. Six of the dozens of hitchhikers he picked up on the roads in and around Santa Cruz County, California never made it to their destinations. Like other serial killers, he blended back into society and into his normal routine, those around him never suspecting he was a cold-blooded killer.

According to the FBI, a "serial murderer" or "serial killer" has behavioral traits that distinguish him from the average murderer. A serial killer murders three or more people with a "cooling off" period in between the murders. In the 1930s, '40s and '50s the term "serial murderer" wasn't part of our language. That being said, in 1853 the term "serial murders" was used by the *New York Times*[179] to describe several violent killings on board a ship. The article related, "...shocking details of another of those serial murders on board ship, arising out of the odious Coolie trade." More than a century would pass before the term was commonly used.

The term "serial murderer" wasn't used in the modern sense until the early 1960s and "serial killer" was popularized only in the 1970s. Of course, that doesn't mean serial killers weren't active before that time period; it simply means the crime hadn't yet been given a formal description. When sexual assault was involved with a murder (which is usually the case with serial murderers), the perpetrator was sometimes referred to as a "sex fiend," a term that came into popular usage in the 1930s. The use of the word "monster" and "fiend" to describe these violent killers goes back much further. Jack the Ripper, sometimes referred to as the "The

Whitechapel Fiend," has been one of the most notorious examples of a serial murderer ever since he started killing prostitutes in London in 1888, and his legend is known worldwide. It was almost unthinkable that a single person could be responsible for committing so many murders and perpetrating such horrific mutilations in the process. He was a true "monster" and it was the uncommonness of his crimes and their appalling nature that caused his story to be burned into the human psyche.

The United States has had its share of serial killers and they are often given descriptive names that capture the headlines. The Boston Strangler, Green River Killer, the Zodiac Killer, Son of Sam, the Night Stalker and the BTK Killer, who collectively murdered some twelve dozen victims, have become household names. Serial killers have gained a huge amount of attention from the media and from law enforcement. With the hope of gaining an understanding of these monsters, criminologists have studied nearly every aspect of their lives and behaviors including their upbringing, criminal history, their first murder, means and triggers for selecting subsequent victims, modus operandi, travel patterns, the method used to murder the victims, and how and where they dispose of the bodies.

Hunting Styles

One area that criminologists have studied is the type of "hunting style" serial killers use to find their victims. As such, their hunting methods have been examined and several different styles have been identified. A serial killer is, in all respects, a predator and behaves very much like a hunter or trapper, or an animal in search of prey. Four hunting styles have been identified that describe various stalking and hunting techniques.

> *Hunters* are those killers who specifically set out from their residence to look for victims, searching through their awareness space they believe contain suitable targets. This is the most commonly used method of

criminal predators...the crimes of the hunter are generally confined to the offender's city of residence. Conversely, *Poachers* travel outside their home city, or operate from an activity site other than their residence, in the search of targets...*Trollers* are opportunistic killers who do not specifically search for victims, but rather encounter them during the course of other, usually routine activities. Their crimes are often spontaneous, but many serial killers have fantasized and planned their crimes in advance so that they are ready and prepared when the opportunity presents itself...*Trappers* have an occupation or position, such as a nurse or orderly in a hospital, where potential victims come to them. They also entice victims into their homes or other location they control by means of subterfuge.[180]

Given the geographic distances between the disappearances, it is unlikely that Katherine, Paula and Connie were encountered by a *Hunter*, unless he moved his residence over the years. That is not to say a different technique might not have been used and one of the three may have been abducted closer to the killer's residence, but it is unlikely all three were "hunted" in that manner.

It is likely they were encountered by either a *Poacher*, who went out searching away from his residence for a victim, or a *Troller*, who in the course of his daily routine watched for the right opportunity to present itself. Whether actively searching for a victim or patiently waiting for a chance encounter, this individual might have driven along secondary roads checking out hitchhikers for desirable characteristics (that were for some reason meaningful to him) and assessing the immediate environment for the degree of seclusion, presence of witnesses, escape routes, etc. In either case, he would have been prepared for such an opportunity, perhaps with a story line he had practiced before so as not to appear threatening, and with some sort of restraint mechanism at hand (e.g., tire iron, rope, knife, revolver, bottle of chloroform). He was likely familiar with the roads in the area, including the less-traveled ones, so he had a good idea where he was going to take his victim and what he was going to do with her when he was done.

Our hypothetical serial killer may not have been specifically hunting for victims on the days Katherine, Paula and Connie disappeared. But, he may have had the opportunity to drive secondary roads along the western New England border with ease, seizing opportunities as they arose. Perhaps his occupation allowed him the freedom needed to perpetrate a crime without having to punch a timecard or to report into work at an appointed hour. His freedom of movement combined with the right opportunity may have dictated his actions rather than any employment restrictions. Examination of the time of year, day of the week, and time of day the disappearances occurred doesn't provide any enlightenment nor does it provide a pattern that would allow us to speculate as to the type of job the abductor might have had. Katherine Hull disappeared sometime after lunch on a Thursday in April, Paula Welden during late afternoon on a Sunday in December, and Connie Smith on a Wednesday in July around 8:45 in the morning.

Attack Methods

Besides hunting techniques, the method of attack has been studied as well.[181] Unfortunately, with only one skeleton found and no indication of the location of the crime scenes it is difficult to identify the exact attack method used. The most common type of offender is referred to as a *Raptor* and makes his attack immediately upon encountering his victim. It occurs where and when his activity space intersects hers. A *Stalker* encounters his victim and follows her until the right circumstances and conditions for an attack coalesce. He moves into her world and activity space as opposed to attacking her when the two of them encounter one another or after he has lured her into his world. Again, our theoretical murderer would not likely be classified as a *Stalker*, given the manner in which Katherine, Paula and Connie disappeared.

An *Ambusher* entices a victim to a place under his control – perhaps his residence, workplace or somewhere else he feels comfortable – and carries out the attack in the midst of his activity space where he feels safest. The three victims were likely drawn with ease right into the killer's vehicle, a space over which he had complete control. He alone determined what direction he would drive and where and when he would stop the vehicle. Whether the victims were attacked immediately after entering the vehicle, as a *Raptor* would have done, or were lured into a false sense of security and brought to another location and then ambushed is unknowable at this point in time.

Serial killer Ted Bundy used victim approach methods that could have been used in the Hull - Welden - Smith disappearances. Sometimes, Bundy would pretend he had an injury - a broken arm or walking with the aid of crutches – and would engage the victim in conversation. He would ask her to help carry his books or to help retrieve a fictional sailboat, and would then offer to give her a ride. But other times, Bundy would pick up his next victim when driving along and passing a hitchhiker. If she met his "criteria," he would pull over and offer her a ride. As soon as his victims entered his car, he would immediately assault them with a crowbar rendering them unconscious, handcuff them, and would drive them away in his Volkswagen. He would then strangle them, sexually assaulting them before or after he murdered them. Most of his victims were high school students and college-age women, though the youngest was age twelve and the oldest age twenty-six.

FBI Classifications

The FBI has developed a system for classifying all types of crimes based on the nature of the offense and the behaviors exhibited by the perpetrator before, during and after the execution of a crime. In their *Crime Classification Manual*, "serial killer" is not listed as a separate category. These types of murders are covered under other headings including Organized Sexual Homicide and Disorganized Sexual Homicide. These broad categories are useful to law enforcement when describing a crime and help them understand the type of individual who committed it.

Organized killers typically plan their murders and their escape, prepare for the attack on their victim by bringing restraints and a weapon, and often use a vehicle in the commission of the crime. "Often he takes his victims to another location and disposes the body in such a manner that it may never be found. The killer is methodical and orderly in his crime. There are usually three separate crime scenes: where the victim was confronted, where the victim was killed, and where the victim's body was disposed."[182] Organized killers tend to be socially skilled, improve their methods over time and are usually interested in media accounts of their crimes.

Disorganized killers might murder spontaneously without planning or preparation and often kill with any weapon that happens to be nearby. They often don't travel very far from their home to commit the crime, are less intelligent than their organized counterparts, and are more socially inept. "The victim's body is usually left where the confrontation and attack took place, and the killer makes no attempt to hide it…He makes little or no effort to cover his tracks, destroy evidence, disguise himself, or develop an escape plan."[183] Disorganized killers don't pay much attention to their crimes in the media and do little to avoid being caught.

There is little doubt that our possible serial killer would fall into the "organized" category. He had the ability to travel long distances, had a vehicle at his disposal, and made sure that his victims' bodies weren't easily found. Organized murderers often make efforts to improve their craft over time. He may have learned from the Katherine Hull murder to hide his victims' bodies better so that Paula Welden, Connie Smith, and perhaps others wouldn't be accidentally found by a group of deer hunters.

Geographic Profiling

The profiling of the movements of the perpetrator in his search for victims has led into a new field of criminology. Geographic Profiling is a relatively recent tool used by law enforcement agencies when studying serial crimes – especially arsons, rapes and murders. The analysis of crime data assists them in determining if there are patterns that can help predict future crimes. In the case of a serial killer, this tool might help predict where bodies are buried, provide guidance as to where a perpetrator might live or work, or where he might engage in recreational activities.

There are several locations of interest when performing a geographic profile of a serial killer's activities – where the victim was last seen, the site where the perpetrator initially came into contact with the victim, where the victim was assaulted, the location of the actual murder, and where the body was disposed. The more crime locations that can be identified the more likely a given crime will be solved. One study[184] found that if four or more of the five locations are known, 85% of the murders are solved. Anything less, and the percentage of crimes solved drops to around 14%. This is one reason the three disappearances (probable murders) were never solved. With so few critical sites identified, the chances of solving the cases were near zero.

In the Hull-Welden-Smith disappearances, assuming they met their fate at the hands of a serial killer, very little is known about these critical locations. Basically, we know approximately where each of the victims was last seen alive – Katherine Hull probably on Columbia Turnpike in the vicinity of Bernie Richmond's store, Paula Welden near Viola Maxwell's house on the Long Trail, and Connie

CLUELESS IN NEW ENGLAND

Smith at the intersection of Belgo Road and Route 44. We also know where one of the bodies was found – on the slope of West Mountain. But exactly where each victim first encountered her killer, where each young woman was taken and assaulted, where the murder was carried out, and where two of the bodies were disposed are unknown data points. Unfortunately, this makes formal geographic profiling analysis impossible to calculate.

A very simple (and admittedly simplistic) geographical analysis of the three disappearances makes use of a geographic "spatial mean" of the three sites where Katherine, Paula and Connie were last seen. The approximate latitude and longitude were determined for the victim-last-seen sites. The average geographic position of the three locations is on the western edge of the city of Pittsfield, Massachusetts, in Pittsfield State Forest. It is under two miles south southeast of the western slope of West Mountain where Katherine's remains were found. It is a point, as the crow flies, about thirty-four miles south of Bennington, and approximately the same distance north of Lakeville. The spatial mean is a convenient way to look at all the cases and to formulate some hypotheses about the general area the killer might have lived, worked and hunted, and for examining the routes he might have traveled. The spatial mean itself doesn't indicate to us where he resided; it just helps us get our hands around the area in which he was active.

Another simple method of analyzing the geographic parameters in a crime series is referred to as the "Circle Hypothesis." A circle connecting the most distant crimes attributed to a serial criminal provides a rough estimate of the area where the perpetrator resides. This technique was used in the present book as a way to search for similar cases. A circle connecting the sites where Paula Welden and Connie Smith were last seen helped define a geographic area in which newspaper and police references to disappearances of other hitchhikers might be found. The circle technique led directly to the Katherine Hull case.

Researchers in England have employed this same technique to estimate where serial criminals of various types live. Using known serial criminals and their geographic range of activities, researchers found that 87% of serial rapists in England resided within the circle of their most distant crimes. It was also true of 82% of arsonists in Australia and 86% of serial killers studied in the United States.[185]

The circle hypothesis applied to the Hull – Welden – Smith cases yields an area encompassing over 3,800 square miles, reaching from Woodford Hollow to Belgo Road, and from the far side of Albany, New York to Northampton, Mass. Granted, this area includes large tracts of forested land, but it is nonetheless a formidable expanse in which to look for a killer. If Paula was abducted by a different individual than involved in the Katherine and Connie cases, the circle connecting Lebanon Springs and Lakeville would be considerably smaller with the spatial mean near the New York border in Great Barrington, Massachusetts.

There are other factors critical to understanding a killer's home and hunting environment. D. Kim Rossmo[186] identified the most relevant factors needed to develop a geographic profile in addition to encounter and crime locations. The profiler would want to know the number of offenders; this is unknown in all three cases. He would also want to understand the population and demographics of the area near the crime locations. The locations where the disappearances occurred were rural with small populations but had larger towns and cities within a few miles. If one simply guesses the residential location of the serial killer based on population and centrality, Pittsfield was (and still is) the most populated city in the area.

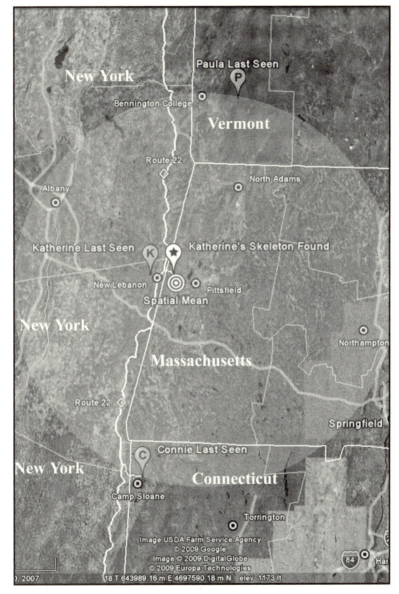

Spatial Mean and Locations of Three Disappearances
Google Earth

A geographic profiler would also want to know the victim's routine activities. This is an interesting problem since all three victims were out of their normal element and doing things not in their daily routine. Katherine had just arrived from Syracuse for vacation in Lebanon Springs and went for a walk, Paula had gone exploring a trail that was unfamiliar to her, and Connie had left camp and was heading toward Lakeville center where she probably hadn't been before. All three had broken their normal routines and were in unfamiliar surroundings.

A description of the landscape and geography where victims were found, access roads and highways, physical boundaries, and terrain are additional factors that help the geographic profiler calculate probable residence of a serial killer. The geography and road network is certainly distinctive along the western New England border. A ridge of mountains acts as a barrier dividing New York from New England. On either side of the mountains are two state roads that run north and south – New York's Route 22 to the west and Route 7 to the east (running through Connecticut, Massachusetts and Vermont). Along the border there are periodic cross-roads that traverse the mountains. Some are main roads used by most traffic, but others – Lebanon Springs Road (off which Katherine Hull was found) and Belgo Road (where Connie Smith was last seen) - are much less used secondary or tertiary roads. Near Bennington, Route 9 (a frequently used road that Paula Welden used to reach the Long Trail) crosses the border into New York State and connects to Route 22 via New York Route 7.

Another factor Rossmo considers critical would be any psychological boundaries that might alter the movements of a perpetrator. This factor became evident when James Scace, who was with the hunting party that found Katherine Hull's skeleton, was hard-pressed to identify any geographic landmarks over the border in New York State even though it was so close to his home. New York is one state and Massachusetts is another. If one lives in Massachusetts, one orients his life, movements and mental maps around his home state. An invisible state line can cause a psychological barrier for many people. Perhaps our alleged serial killer intuitively understood this phenomenon and knew that when police would start searching, most of the early efforts would be in the state where the victim disappeared, stopping at the borders. Later, when local search efforts proved unproductive, investigators and searchers crossed state lines looking for clues.

The lapse between the time when a victim was last seen and when the body was found is also critical. If both events occur within twenty-four hours, and the distance separating the two sites is less than 200 feet, there is a fairly high likelihood of solving the murder. If the time lapse is more than a month and the two sites are greater than $1\frac{1}{2}$ miles from one another, the probability of solving a case nears zero. In the Hull - Welden - Smith cases, the three victims were likely picked up while hitchhiking, probably subdued and driven miles away very quickly. Finding Katherine Hull's remains seven years later on a mountainside several miles from where she was last seen, and with no remains found for the other two victims, it was pretty much guaranteed the three cases would never be solved.

The Katherine Hull case is different from the others in that her remains were found only a few miles from where she was last seen entering someone's car. The FBI has claimed that a serial murderer's first crime in the series is often closer to his home than later ones. If true in this series of crimes, and if Katherine Hull was the first victim, then the residence of the killer would possibly be closer to where Katherine disappeared than where Paula Welden and Connie Smith were last seen. Serial killers would behave this way for several reasons – they would draw attention away from their area of residence and they would expand their potential hunting ground. Often, there is a "buffer zone" that exists around the perpetrator's residence, not committing crimes too close to home so as not to draw attention to himself. This is not to say crimes are never committed within this zone but the risk of being caught is considerably higher for the perpetrator. Also, in a community where multiple crimes are committed, there is an increased vigilance on the part of the public and law enforcement. Young women disappearing over forty miles away, in different states don't have the same effect on a community or pressure on law enforcement agencies to solve the case as three women vanishing near one another.

Psychological Motives

One of the other factors that make it difficult to solve murders committed by serial killers is that they generally target strangers. In more run-of-the-mill murders, police determine the suspects who might have a motive. Usually the list is short and focuses on those involved in a love triangle, anyone who recently argued with the victim, an angry spouse, individuals who would benefit financially, acquaintances of the victim who might have a vendetta, etc. In most serial cases, these traditional types of motives are non-existent. The motives of serial killers are often complex, internalized and psychosexually based. Victims are selected seemingly at random – though they meet some sort of criteria determined by the killer. With no prior relationship between the murderer and victim, it is difficult to determine why the victim was chosen.

Sexual serial killers have been broken down into categories that describe their motives and behaviors. One type of sexual murderer, *power-assertive*, is motivated by exercising power over his victim – beating and raping her before he takes complete control over her life by murdering her. A *power-reassurance* killer is more fantasy driven and acts out some sort of sexual fantasy while raping his victim. When the victim interrupts his fantasy by fighting back, the rapist resorts to murder and may try to fulfill his fantasy after the death of the victim. Perhaps the most horrifying type of serial killer, *anger-excitation*, is one that terrorizes his victim before he murders her. For him, the process leading up to the murder is more important than the murder itself, and he often continues his fantasies afterward through mutilation of the victim.

The last of the sexual serial killer categories relates to taking out anger on a victim and is referred to as *anger-retaliatory*. The killer seeks revenge against someone who has in some way disrespected or rejected him. Often, rather than taking his revenge directly against the woman who is the subject of his anger, he takes his rage out against a surrogate. For example, when serial rapist-murderer Monte Rissell's girlfriend sent him a letter in 1975 breaking up with him, he drove to her college campus, parked his car and eventually observed her accompanied by another man. He did nothing at that time and returned to his apartment in Alexandria, Virginia, where he sat in his car and waited. In the early morning hours, another young woman parked her car and Rissell took his displaced revenge. Rissell abducted her and raped her before he murdered her. He continued to take out his revenge against his former girlfriend by killing four more women before he was finally caught.

One can make a case that some of the circumstances and timing surrounding the disappearance of Paula Welden could indicate an *anger-retaliatory* motive. Shortly after Paula walked by the house where Alfred Gadette was arguing with Viola Maxwell, Gadette stormed away in a jealous rage. Depending on which of Gadette's stories can be believed, he either went across the street to the shack where he spent the rest of the night, or he drove up the Long Trail in his truck. There is a possibility that he could have displaced his jealous rage upon an unsuspecting and innocent substitute for his girlfriend whom he suspected was cheating on him. He was a suspect of investigators at two different times but they couldn't find any evidence implicating him, and there was no body to be found. Gadette did tell friends he knew within 100 feet where Paula was buried, but later said he was only joking. Now deceased, he was the only named person of interest in this case even though no physical evidence was ever uncovered.

One perplexing issue regarding the three disappearances relates to the time that elapsed between the events. Katherine disappeared in 1936, Paula in 1946, and Connie in 1952. The crimes of serial killers have been known to span over many years and often have periods of inactivity, called "remission" by criminologists. These periods can be a function of psychological reasons, incarceration for other crimes, moving his residence or his job, or something beyond his control. For example, World War II was being fought during four of the years between Katherine and Paula's disappearances. Katherine's murderer could have been in the armed forces during some of those years, which put his interest in hitchhikers on hold – at least in western New England.

Another possibility is he may have moved from place to place making him a migratory predator. Perhaps his occupation took him to other states where he practiced his craft. He may well have been active in other jurisdictions during the seeming gaps of time between the Hull-Welden-Smith disappearances.

Body Disposal

Where and how a serial killer disposes of a body has considerable significance to investigators. Some are left out in the open for investigators to find readily, some are discarded like trash, some are thrown into a body of water to help destroy physical evidence, and others are hidden (sometimes buried in a shallow grave) to prevent investigators from finding them. One study[187] shed some light on body disposal methods and concluded:

> The method of handling and leaving the victim's body will also offer insight into the victim's relationship to the killer. A victim left clothed or in

an area allowing easy discovery suggest she was "loved" by the killer. A well-treated, and easily found victim may also signify a killer who has a religious upbringing and who does not feel a rage directed at the victim or at society.

A victim who is left in a remote area with no care taken to bury the body suggests that the killer had little regard for her. Once she served his needs he only sought to dispose of her to avoid detection. It also suggests that the killer admits that he will continue to kill and that he hopes to deter police recognition of his activity.

Whether Katherine Hull was murdered near the site where her body was found or killed elsewhere and her body dumped on West Mountain is unknown. If she was killed elsewhere, there would have been a large amount of forensic evidence at the murder site, whether it be in a car, someone's home or perhaps another area of woods. But unless a suspect had been identified the chance of uncovering that site was negligible. With the passage of years, the natural elements destroyed most of the evidence at the site where Katherine's skeleton was found.

Even though the physical evidence is gone, the behavioral evidence is still with us. The fact that Katherine's body was hidden off an isolated road indicates her murderer was trying to prevent searchers, police, and anyone else from finding her. And, if the study on body disposal is accurate, the manner in which he disposed of her body indicates he intended to continue to kill.

Chance Encounters

The probability that Paula Welden might have encountered a murderer on the Long Trail was unsettling to former Vermont state policeman John "Skip" Fagerholm. Although he didn't investigate the Welden case, and didn't join the Vermont State Police until

1977, he became fascinated by the mystery surrounding it. Fagerholm wrote a newspaper article[188] near the fiftieth anniversary of Paula's last walk in which he stated, "Those that speculate that it was a murder can not be disproven. However, the chances that a homicidal maniac was also wandering the Long Trail on December 1 at night and encountering the college student make me place my money on the theory of lost in some very large woods never to be found again." In one sense he is correct. The probability of any random person encountering a homicidal monster at a specific place and point in time is very small. Yet it happens every day, when someone is murdered by a complete stranger.

In order to understand the probability, one needs to look at it from the murderer's point of view. A serial murderer has a multitude of victims from whom to choose. He may roam city streets searching for human prey who possess a certain "look," or he may drive back-roads trolling for hitchhikers who will freely and willingly enter his car – all he has to do is pull over and stop. The probability is quite high that one of the people he encounters in this manner will be his next victim. By hitchhiking and being by themselves outside their safety zones, Katherine, Paula, and Connie placed themselves in a potentially perilous environment. In one sense, they were random victims. But in another sense, they may have inadvertently made themselves part of a small subset of potential victims to one or more murderers who were in a hunting frame of mind. Dozens of other "random" potential victims were likely considered and passed over for one reason or another. It is the fact that Katherine, Paula, and Connie disappeared that is the reason they are still being discussed. We don't even know the names of the other potential victims who went on to live their lives never knowing how very lucky they were.

Chapter VI

*"But O for the touch of a vanished hand,
    And the sound of a voice that is still!"*

Alfred Lord Tennyson, *Break, Break, Break*

CLUELESS IN NEW ENGLAND

Secluded Roads

Given the similarities among the cases, the question arises whether the disappearances of Katherine Hull, Paula Welden and Connie Smith could be related to one another. The evidence is certainly circumstantial with similar events surrounding their disappearances – trusting young women hitchhiking along country roads near the western border of New England and who disappeared as if their abductor never wanted them found. It is possible the three disappearances represent only a small part of an unknown killer's corpus of work. Related cases may exist among the thousands of unsolved crimes in the Northeast. Police departments in New England and New York State within the Bennington - Lakeville circle and beyond might consider looking through their dusty files for cold murder cases, unsolved rapes, missing persons, and attempted abductions from the same time frame. And perhaps local historians can search through crumbling clippings in scrapbooks, rarely used rolls of microfilm, and databases of digitized newspapers seeking out similar unsolved crimes or disappearances. There may be a single clue amidst those long-forgotten crimes that will finally help solve some of the most intriguing cold cases in the Northeast.

Often, murderers are interviewed as potential suspects in the course of investigations but there is no hard evidence pointing to them. There are a couple of adages used by law enforcement personnel that are apropos. First, "If you want the name of your murderer, just look in the case file." There is a good chance he was interviewed either as a witness or a suspect. Second, in the case of a serial crime, "If you solve one you solve them all." Since there are no official records for the Katherine Hull case, it is impossible to compare names that might be common in all three cases. Comparing the names of those interviewed from the Paula Welden and Connie Smith case files revealed no commonality in the names of suspects or witnesses. Even though there are no names common in the Welden - Smith case files, there is a possibility that a name in one of the files may have a connection to the other cases.

Some serial killers and even one-time murderers have been known to somehow insert themselves into the investigation of their crimes. Like the arsonist who watches the fire he set, sometimes the murderer is in the crowd that gathers when a body is discovered, assists in a search for a missing person when he already knows where the body can be found, or strikes up conversations with investigators about the crime. One such case near Saranac Lake in 1934 related to the murder of 14-year-old Cleo Tellstone. The girl was abducted by Thomas Frederick Showers, a Civilian Conservation Corp worker, in the town of Franklin, New York. He murdered Cleo and dumped her body in deep woods over two miles from her home. Showers admitted to the crime and investigators discovered he had been part of the 200-person search party that looked for the girl. Coincidentally, Showers' permanent residence was in Syracuse, about three miles from Katherine Hull's home, and he committed his murder only a few miles from her father's home in Saranac Lake. He would have made a good suspect in Katherine's probable murder but was in jail at the time of her disappearance. It would be enlightening if one could compare lists of searchers for the Hull, Welden and Smith cases to determine if any of the same names appear. Unfortunately, lists of searchers do not seem to have been created in the first place and none have been located.

In examining cases from fifty-plus years ago certain patterns began to emerge. Though each disappearance has its own unique set of circumstances, there is a surprising amount of similarity in how the investigations unfolded. When a young woman or girl disappeared hitchhiking along quiet roads the first assumption made by friends, family, college administrators and camp directors was that she might be found in the immediate vicinity or had become lost in nearby woods. Small-scale searches were conducted before the police were called in, resulting in significant delays in investigating other possible explanations for the disappearance. The possibility of foul play was often one of the last lines of inquiry.

Once law enforcement became involved - about six to eight hours after Katherine waved her final goodbye to her father; about twenty-one hours after Paula was last seen on the Long Trail; and about three hours after Connie was noticed missing by her tent mates - more formal searches were undertaken and statements were sought from witnesses. Then, search parties comprised of campers, students, local residents, law enforcement officials, family members, and Boy Scouts were formed. Later, National Guard troops, air support, trained dogs, and searchers on horseback were brought in to search more distant, expansive areas of terrain. It is likely Katherine, Paula and Connie were murdered at the hands of a sick-minded killer before they were even reported missing to the police. Although foul play was eventually considered a possibility in all three cases, the initial expenditure of time and effort revolved around searching the nearby woods for a lost young woman.

When searchers had no success, the search area was expanded and bulletins were put out to police departments in neighboring states and beyond. Local newspapers printed articles about the disappearance and the stories were then picked up by national news services. As news articles appeared in cities distant from the disappearance, "sightings" of the missing individual were reported. Before long, police received letters from cranks or crooks who speculated as to what happened, and from others who asserted to have some knowledge of the case. Inevitably, psychics became involved in trying to locate the missing individual, usually claiming they "know" she is still alive. Family and friends in situations like these were, and still are, understandably, willing to try anything to get their loved ones back, no matter how unconventional the means might be. Rarely are psychics of any real help, though on occasion they have pointed to an area that hasn't been searched. Then came the inevitable confessions of guilt by criminals or unbalanced persons who sought some sort of spotlight.

Finally, when no new news was being reported and all the clues had been tracked down without any luck, newspapers and other media stopped covering the story. As a result, the number of "sightings" diminished, the number people claiming some sort of knowledge of the case decreased, and more importantly, public awareness of the case faded away. In the Paula Welden and Connie Smith cases in particular, family members kept the story alive for many months through their involvement, persistence and tenacity. They worked beside law enforcement in the search and were active in determining the course of the investigations. Family and police also kept news reporters informed of new developments and of new avenues of investigation. This served to keep their readers interested in the case, provided news editors a reason for continuing to cover it, and kept the missing person's story in the public eye. Unfortunately, no matter how much press coverage was given in the Welden – Smith cases, no favorable results were ever achieved.

Another pattern emerged relating to the perception of what happened to the missing person. The first assumption when Katherine, Paula and Connie were discovered missing was that they were lost in the woods or may have been lying injured nearby. When searches were unsuccessful and no clues were uncovered, the possibility that they ran away with friends or headed home due to homesickness became the focus of the investigations. Later, the possibility that they had joined a convent or had run away with a young man gained the attention of investigators. Then, the speculation that the missing woman was depressed often led to the possibility of suicide being considered. In some of these types of cases, suicide was how they ended, but it is certainly not true in all of them. Unfortunately, comments from friends that the missing person had recently been gloomy, or depressed, or unhappy, or overly happy, suddenly loom large as the reason someone disappeared and might be suicidal. This was particularly true in the Paula Welden case, but people don't normally commit suicide by intentionally walking into the woods and dying of exposure.

Many unsolved missing person cases were attributed to "amnesia." There had been several widely publicized cases[189] of highly respected people leaving their homes suddenly and turning up months later in a different community, working at a different occupation, with a different identity. When they were found they had no recollection of their former life, though with the passage of time and psychological therapy they regained their original identity. The public was fascinated with the phenomenon but at the same time many people were dubious of the claims. Some people who disappeared for a few days or weeks seemed to mimic the symptoms when they returned home and may simply have been using the diagnosis as a means of hiding some indiscretion.

The belief by family and friends that their loved one who disappeared may have been suffering from the condition was most likely a reflection of their hopeful feelings that she was still alive. They envisioned her as not remembering who she was or where she was from, and roaming about in some nearby city and possibly even starting a new life and identity. This scenario offered the family some solace that their loved one might return home someday. Amnesia became a possible explanation in many missing person cases, though in fact it is a very rare event and seldom obliterates a person's entire past.

Katherine Hull's parents were hopeful of just such a situation and held on to that possibility until her skeleton was found in 1943.

In some ways, they must have been relieved by the discovery but it undoubtedly raised more questions about how she ended up on a remote slope of West Mountain. After Katherine's disappearance her family moved apart. Minnie split her time between Lebanon Springs and Florida and died in 1952. Harry Hull spent much of his time at his cabin at Rainbow Lake in upstate New York and in Allendale, Florida, dying there in 1958. Florence lived in Syracuse and also wintered in Florida. She died in 1968, nearly 32 years after Katherine's disappearance.

Katherine's sister Marjorie lived in her home on Lancaster Avenue in Syracuse for the rest of her life. After her father died, she inherited the property on Rainbow Lake and changed the name of her street from Lake Road to Hull Road. Upon her death in 1996, Marjorie donated more than $350,000 to Clarkson University in Potsdam, New York, to establish a scholarship in honor of her family. The Harry and Florence P. Hull and Katherine E. Hull Endowed Scholarship provides funds for qualified undergraduate students in the engineering program. With Marjorie's death, the entire family was again reunited in the Cemetery of the Evergreens in Lebanon Springs.

The investigators in the Paula Welden case also speculated she may have developed amnesia. Fortunately for the state of Vermont, its legislators didn't suffer the same malady nor forgot the stir caused by Paula's disappearance. They responded loud and clear to the criticisms regarding the state's handling of the case by instituting the Vermont State Police.

On July 1, 1947, seven months after Paula took her last walk, Vermont started to be patrolled by a professionally trained police force. Thirty-four men graduated from a six-week police training course and reported to Brigadier General Merritt A. Edson, former Marine Corp staff officer and recipient of the Congressional Medal of Honor for service on Guadalcanal. The legislature had debated the subject for ten years and the state's sheriffs had argued against the formation of such an organization since 1937.

It took the disappearance of Paula Welden and the criticisms leveled by her father and others to convince the legislature of the need for a formally trained law enforcement agency operating at the state level. They finally set aside the parochial interests of the sheriffs in consideration of the public good. As a direct result of Paula's disappearance, the Vermont State Police to this day have the responsibility for all wilderness search and rescue missions.

Regarding the formation of the Vermont State Police, Mr. Welden stated, "If my daughter has been murdered, as I feel she has been, there is consolation in the fact that her dying has spurred Vermonters into the establishment of a new state police organization which may serve to protect the lives and welfare of their own children."[190] On the twentieth anniversary of Paula's disappearance, a reporter contacted Welden at his retirement home in Englewood, Florida. He was surprised to have anyone ask about the case after all those years; it had been eighteen years since he had been contacted by anyone, including the police. When asked what he believed happened to his daughter, he replied he was convinced "she had met with foul play. Not on any fact, but on the knowledge that that is the answer in most such cases."[191]

Peter Smith didn't forget either. In November 1984, Connie's father visited Lakeville one more time to search for Connie. He hadn't been back in twenty-five years but was in New York on business and decided to visit the area where his daughter had disappeared. During his visit, he told the *Lakeville Journal*'s then cub reporter Brigitte Ruthman, "I think of her when I see a tall woman walk by who would be about her age. It's a perpetual hope that something will turn up. The alternative to giving up at this late date is faint hope. I had to come back to see the camp again. I made the trip to satisfy something inside me."[192]

Others remember Connie to this day. Trooper Richard Chapman worked on the case on his own for more than a decade after Connie disappeared. In 1984, he reflected, "I think of Connie quite often. The whole mystery has played on my mind ever since."[193] Brigitte Ruthman has written several other articles about the baffling case since she first met Connie's father. When she interviewed Chapman in 2009, he confided to her his only regret[194] from his 24-year career with the Connecticut State Police:

"I never found Connie."

In spite of all the foot and air searching, interviews conducted, consultations with psychics, false confessions, sightings in distant cities, speculations, lie detector tests, leads that led only to dead ends, dashed hopes, and the passage of time, we are still left in the dark as to what transpired on the back-roads and trails along the mountains in western New England. What happened to Paula Welden and Connie Smith and where are their bodies? After all that has been done and said, investigators in the Welden and Smith cases believed, and still believe, the two were likely abducted and murdered.

Based on the assumption that the two cases could be related to one another, and are also associated with the disappearance of Katherine Hull, we can look at the Welden - Smith cases in a new light. So let us theorize that Katherine was picked up while hitchhiking, taken to some unknown location, probably sexually assaulted, eventually murdered, and her body dumped off the Lebanon Springs Road on West Mountain in Hancock, Massachusetts. The Katherine Hull case offers us an unprecedented opportunity to learn from the circumstances surrounding her demise and applying that knowledge to the other two cases.

Clueless in New England

The exact location where Katherine was last seen alive is uncertain. Newspaper articles cite witness accounts that she was hitchhiking and at some unknown point entered an automobile. We do know that general store owner Bernie Richmond saw her walk by. It is likely Katherine thumbed a ride to the center of New Lebanon and equally likely she would have thumbed a ride back. For lack of a better reference, Richmond's store was the last sighting that can be used to pinpoint her location - the intersection of Route 20 and Mill Road in New Lebanon - about $3\frac{1}{2}$ miles from Katherine's grandmother's house. At some point in time after being seen by Bernie Richmond, she was likely picked up by a driver who saw Katherine with her thumb extended. Perhaps there was something about her that reminded him of someone who had made him angry or something about her teased some sexual fantasy. An unsuspecting Katherine Hull climbed into his automobile not knowing that this complete stranger had already decided her fate.

The next thing we know for certain is that Katherine's skeleton was found under a hemlock tree on West Mountain. The location of her body was a little more than four miles away (as the crow flies) and a little more than five miles away if one were to drive the most direct route – the same route Katherine may have taken from her grandmother's house. The driver may have gone north on Route 22 to Main Street in Lebanon Springs, perhaps having offered Katherine a ride to her grandmother's home and, instead of taking a left on Spring Hill Road, continued up the secluded Lebanon Springs Road where he carried out his self-appointed mission. The driver of the automobile or truck would have been familiar with the mountain roads and the access paths that led up the hill toward the telephone lines near the area where the skeleton was found. He may have been a hunter familiar with the area or perhaps had even worked in the construction of the telephone lines. He could have been a worker with the Civilian Conservation Corps and knew every square inch of the mountains. Or, he may have been a truck driver who knew all the roads and alternate routes in the area.

With darkness falling, Paula Welden was last seen walking up the Long Trail by Viola Maxwell and Fred Gadette in the heat of their argument. For about two miles, the Long Trail was drivable – now called Harbour Road - and had houses and shelters along the way. Viola's house was about a half mile from the upper end of the road portion of the trail. At the uppermost part of the hard-packed dirt road, the easily drivable portion ended and the trail continued through quickly darkening woods. Paula was an intelligent woman and it is unlikely she would have ventured very far into the woods at that time of day with dusk falling.

Paula likely had satisfied her curiosity about the location of the Long Trail and decided to return some day in the near future with her hiking friends. In all likelihood, she turned around and started to walk back down the drivable portion of the road and either accepted a ride from someone driving on the trail or walked down to the intersection of Route 9 and flipped out her thumb. Perhaps an angry Alfred Gadette, or the unidentified driver of the half-ton pick-up truck with New York plates seen on the Long Trial (and who was "cleared" by Sheriff W. Clyde Peck) offered her a ride. It seems unlikely that a rapist/murderer would drive his victim toward a relatively populated area such as Bennington center so it is unlikely he would have driven Paula to the west. Heading east on Route 9 would offer him a much better alternative for a secluded place to carry out his crimes.

Examination of the areas searched in the Paula Welden case reveals shortcomings in the way the search patterns were undertaken. Besides the Bennington College campus and surrounding area, the search efforts in 1946 and 1947 explored a swath of the Long Trail extending 8-10 miles north from Route 9; into Bickford Hollow that veers off to the northwest of the trail; up the Blue Trail running north of the Draper Manufacturing Company (a short distance west of the Long Trail); on the eastern and western slopes of Bald Mountain to the west; along Hell Hollow (running east of the Long Trail for about two miles); down the Long Trail south of Route 9 over Harmon Hill as far as Sucker Pond (now Lake Hancock); and south of Route 9 in the Dunville Hollow region. The approach to Everett's Cave on Mount Anthony (southwest of Bennington center), a swamp in Manchester where screams were thought to emanate, and the length of Route 9 from Bennington to Brattleboro were also searched.

There is no mention in news accounts that the area east (except for Hell Hollow) or northeast of the Long Trail was searched at all. More importantly, all the searches were conducted with the idea in mind that Paula had gotten lost while hiking and may have taken a wrong turn on the Long Trail. For the most part, the searches concentrated on the trails heading in the direction she was last seen walking. Ground searches based on the assumption she had been abducted and had gone in a different direction, and not on foot, were never conducted.

There is one area in that direction – east on Route 9 - that is similar to the area where Katherine Hull's skeleton was found. A seldom used, secluded, dirt road/trail leads into the mountains toward Little Pond, which is located about $2\frac{1}{2}$ miles northeast of the section of the Long Trail where Paula was last seen. There are actually two trails leading to Little Pond (with the Forest Service road designations FR 275 and FR 272) and starting at Route 9. Whether these trails were drivable in 1946 is uncertain, but it is known that today the trails from Route 9 are maneuverable with an all-terrain vehicle.

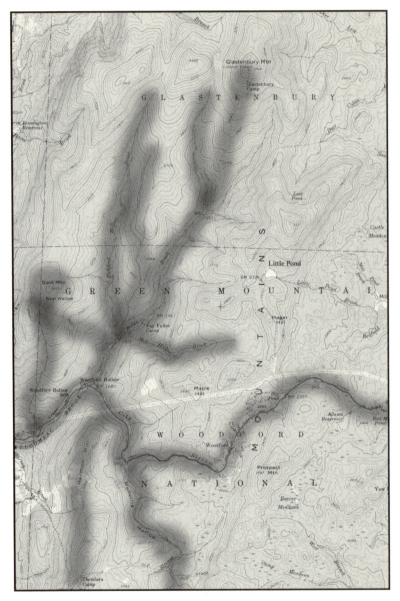

Shaded Areas Show Approximate Primary Search Areas
Bennington Quadrangle, USGS Map, 1954

CLUELESS IN NEW ENGLAND

The two forest roads/trails leading to Little Pond start about five miles from the Route 9 intersection with Harbour Road and are on the same stretch of road where a couple saw footprints and a single set of tire tracks in the snow when they were putting chains on their tires. The couple noted the footprints ended abruptly after about 400 yards. Could Paula have become disoriented and headed in the wrong direction on her way back to the college, only to have been picked up along Route 9? Or, could she have gotten out of an automobile or truck and tried to walk or run away from danger only to be forced back into the vehicle?

At one time, another trail connected what became known as the Long Trail with Little Pond. The USGS topographical map from 1898 shows a trail starting less than a mile beyond the top of what is now Harbour Road and leading to Little Pond. Again, whether this was drivable in 1946 is unknown, though one local historian believes it would have been too rugged and steep to use a vehicle. The same map shows a dirt road (now FR 275) leading south to what is now Route 9.

Katherine Hull's skeleton was found approximately one-tenth of a mile above the Lebanon Springs Road but only a short distance off an access road to the telephone poles that traversed the mountain. If the two cases are related, or the perpetrators used similar methods, then Paula Welden's killer may have used the same disposal method and dumped, or hidden, or buried her body off the trails that lead toward Little Pond. There may have been other trails or logging roads in the area that would meet the needs of a killer intent on hiding a body so it wouldn't be found. They may not have appeared on topographical maps or road maps but may have been accessible by motor vehicles. From newspaper articles and police reports there is no indication that the areas along the Little Pond roads and trails were ever searched.

MICHAEL C. DOOLING

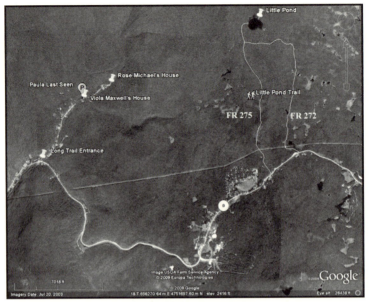

Trail to Little Pond
Google Earth

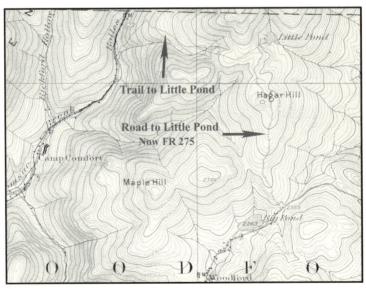

Map Showing Trail and Dirt Road to Little Pond
Bennington Quadrangle, USGS Map, 1898

Clueless in New England

Good intentions and intuition guided the camp staff and the Connecticut State Police in the search for Connie Smith. They initially searched the grounds of Camp Sloane and the area surrounding it. After that, police interviewed witnesses to determine the direction she was heading. Foot and horseback searches were undertaken to various ponds and mine pits, wooded areas, the Rudd Pond area in New York, Mount Riga, Mount Washington and Red Mountain. Significant effort was expended conducting air searches with numerous planes and helicopters – mostly around Lakeville and parts of southwestern Massachusetts and just over the border into New York. If Connie had been walking along a road, lying in a gutter or a field, or fallen into a one of the water-filled ore pits, she likely would have been found. But since it was the middle of summer, the trees were full of foliage and a body disposed of like Katherine Hull's would have been impossible to see from the air. During the ground and air searches, they were primarily looking for a lost girl roaming around the area and it was unlikely they would have found a girl abducted by someone who was intent upon doing her harm and hiding her body.

When Connie disappeared, she was last seen near the intersection of Route 44 and Belgo Road in Lakeville. Within moments of having been seen walking in an easterly direction on the north side of Route 44 by Mrs. Barnett, it is probable a man driving either west on Route 44 or emerging from Belgo Road saw Connie hitchhiking and stopped. He likely asked where she was headed and Connie, unafraid of talking to strangers, told him she was going to the center of Lakeville. He would have offered her a ride and perhaps told her he knew a shortcut. Someone intending harm would likely stay away from downtown Lakeville and probably shy away from the center of Millerton, New York three miles to the west. The last place a would-be killer would want to be is near a population or business center when he has an abductee in his car.

It is possible the perpetrator picked up Connie and drove her straight out Belgo Road, avoiding the centers of Lakeville and Millerton, New York. This road quickly became more secluded and was comprised mostly of farmland, including the 850-acre Shagroy turkey farm. From there, he may have continued into New York on Shagroy Road, headed north on Rudd Pond toward one of the seldom used, secluded, dirt roads that penetrate the Taconic Range. One such road that bears similarities to Lebanon Springs Road is Grassy Pond Drive, an extension of Kaye Road, in the town of North East, New York. It winds around the base of the Taconic range for several miles heading toward South Pond and Grassy Pond to the north. The now private road is about a five-mile drive from where Connie was last seen. There is no evidence in police files or news accounts that this area was searched. Other secluded roads farther north have similar characteristics and could also have been used to dispose of her body.

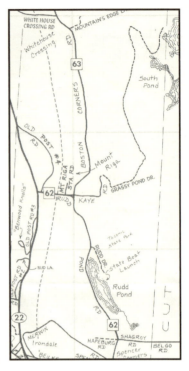

Roads Leading from Belgo Road
Courtesy of Harbor Publications

Another possibility exists that the murderer may have preferred to dispose of the bodies in another area altogether. Some serial killers dump multiple bodies in the same vicinity. It becomes his private graveyard for his victims where he can visit and re-live the excitement he experienced when he murdered each one of them. Serial killer Ted Bundy disposed of the heads of four of his victims in that manner, leaving their skulls on Taylor Mountain in Washington State. One of his victims had disappeared more than 250 miles away from the mountain. The slopes of West Mountain where Katherine Hull's remains were found would be another logical place to search for the remains of other victims. Katherine had remained unfound for seven years in that spot under the hemlock tree and her body hadn't been buried or hidden in any way. It is possible our hypothetical killer returned to this area after Katherine's remains were found to dispose of subsequent victims. Perhaps he did a better job obscuring the bodies, burying them in shallow graves or covering them with brush or rocks.

D. Kim Rossmo,[195] summarized studies of where murderers disposed of the bodies of their victims. He wrote, "Experience and research has shown that a victim's body is unlikely to be carried more than 150 feet from the murder site to the dump site, or more than 150 feet from a vehicle...An adult body dumped in a remote area will usually be found within 50 feet of a road or trail...and a child's body within 200 feet." He recommends, "A search following the road network (or trail network) will therefore be more effective and efficient than a standard grid search." The rule-of-thumb distances mentioned by Rossmo are approximations and there are exceptions.

Katherine Hull was found on West Mountain over 500 feet off the old Lebanon Springs Road but much closer to the access road to the telephone poles (the exact distance isn't known); little Brenda Doucette was left 200 feet off a secluded road in Wolcott, Connecticut; Gaetane Boivin was pushed out of a car into a ditch next to an almost impassable road in Waterbury, Connecticut. Given the behavioral information of killers' body-dumping practices, the bodies of Paula and Connie wouldn't have been disposed of very far off a path, trail or road. And if Alfred Gadette really knew within 100 feet where Paula was buried, he may have used a road or trail as a reference point. If any future searches are ever undertaken, they should account for at least that distance from a road or trail.

When Connecticut's Forensic Anthropologist, Dr. Albert Harper, was asked about the likely condition of a body after more than fifty years, he stated that it depends whether the body was buried or not. If a body is left on the surface of the ground with little or no protection from New England's natural elements, there may be some skeletal remains left, most probably the teeth. It is likely the rest of the remains would be, for the most part, disintegrated. If the body had been buried in a shallow grave, it would be protected somewhat from the elements. After five-plus decades, depending on the acidity of the soil, there may be some skeletal evidence remaining. The likelihood of cadaver-sniffing dogs having the ability to detect such remains is in the words of Dr. Harper, "extremely unlikely."

One possible aid to searchers for Paula Welden exists. When she disappeared, Paula was wearing a gold, Elgin watch with a narrow black band. Although there may be few human remains left or they may be difficult to locate, Paula's watch might be found with the aid of a metal detector. It could still be identifiable by the repairer's mark, "13050 HD," scratched on the inside of the back case.

Chapter VII

"Oh, don't be scared. Nobody's going to hurt you."

Thornton Wilder, *Our Town*

CLUELESS IN NEW ENGLAND

Grover's Corners

As we gaze at the images of Katherine Hull, Paula Welden and Connie Smith, we see their familiar faces, forever frozen in time; their expressions never changing; their faces never aging; their eyes never again looking in wonderment or joy; their features never softening with the wisdom of the years. And something bothers us.

Katherine, Paula and Connie were good, wholesome young women who disappeared while hitchhiking and were most likely murdered by a psychopathic killer. Unlike the victims of many murderers of strangers, they weren't drug addicts, prostitutes, or girls with loose morals. They weren't particularly troubled, didn't live dangerous lifestyles, and other than hitchhiking, didn't engage in risky behaviors. They were, in many ways, innocents who trusted that everyone held the same values of common decency, honesty, and respect that they did. It is unlikely that any one of the three could have imagined that someone nice enough to offer them a ride would ever want to hurt them.

Perhaps it is their familiarity that is most unsettling about the disappearances of these three young women. They are our daughters who we carry as infants and dress in pink outfits with matching bonnets. They are the neighborhood girls who sell us Girl Scout cookies and sit near us in church. They are the youngsters we trustingly send to summer camp to gain independence and the young women for whom we have high hopes when we send them off to college. We all know them. They live in all our towns. That...is what is so bothersome.

CLUELESS IN NEW ENGLAND

There's a Long, Long Trail A-Winding
Lyrics by Stoddard King

Nights are growing very lonely,
    Days are very long;
I'm a-growing weary only
    List'ning for your song.
Old remembrances are thronging
    Thro' my memory.
Till it seems the world is full of dreams
    Just to call you back to me.

All night long I hear you calling,
    Calling sweet and low;
Seem to hear your footsteps falling,
    Ev'ry where I go.
Tho' the road between us stretches
    Many a weary mile.
I forget that you're not with me yet,
    When I think I see you smile.

There's a long, long trail a-winding
    Into the land of my dreams,
Where the nightingales are singing
    And a white moon beams.
There's a long, long night of waiting
    Until my dreams all come true;
Till the day when I'll be going down
    That long, long trail with you

References

Ainslee, Guy. "A Remarkable Case," *Ballou's Monthly Magazine*, January 1893.

Albany Times Union.

Alder, Ken. *The Lie Detectors: The History of an American Obsession.* New York: Free Press, 2007.

Ayers, Captain John H. & Carol Bird. *Missing Men: The Story of the Missing Persons Bureau of the New York Police Department.* Garden City: Garden City Publishing, 1932.

Barber, John Warner. *Connecticut Historical Collections.* New Haven: John W. Barber, 1836.

Bartlett, Ellen Strong. "Salisbury." *The Connecticut Quarterly*, December 1898.

Begg, Paul. *Into Thin Air: People Who Disappear.* Newton Abbot: David & Charles, 1979.

Bennington College Bulletin 1946-1947.

Bennington Evening Banner.

Berkshire Evening Eagle.

Brattleboro Reformer.

Chatham Courier.

Canter, David. *Mapping Murder: The Secrets of Geographical Profiling.* London: Virgin Books, 2003.

Churchill, Allen. *They Never Came Back.* New York: Ace Books, 1960.

Citro, Joseph A. *Green Mountain Ghosts, Ghouls, and Unsolved Mysteries.* Boston: Houghton Mifflin, 1994.

Connecticut: A Guide to its Roads, Lore, People. Boston: Houghton Mifflin, 1938.

Connie Smith Case File, Connecticut State Police Department.

Correspondence with Alvin Miller, former staff member at Camp Sloane.

Crossman, Rev. Joseph W. *New Year's Discourse delivered at Salisbury, on Lord's day, January 2d, 1803 containing the ancient history of the town.* Hartford: Hudson and Goodwin, 1803.

Disturnell, John. *The Traveler's Guide to the Hudson River.* New York: American News Company, 1864.

Fitchburg Sentinel.

Hartford Courant.

Hickey, Eric W. *Serial Murderers and Their Victims.* Belmont, CA: Wadsworth, 2002.

Hudson Daily Star.

Interview and correspondence with James Scace.

Interview with former Connecticut State Policeman Richard G. Chapman.

Jones, Barbara. *Bennington College: The Development of an Educational Idea.* New York: Harper & Brothers, 1946.

Keene Evening Sentinel.

Knickerbocker Press.

Lakeville Journal.

Life Magazine.

Mail-A-Map Street Map of North East, Amenia & Millerton. Madison, CT: Harbor Publications, 2008

Massachusetts State Police Laboratory Logbook, 1943.

McFarland, Gerald. *The Counterfeit Man: The True Story of the Boorn-Colvin Murder Case.* New York: Pantheon Books, 1990.

New York Times.

North Adams Evening Transcript.

Paula Welden Case File, Vermont State Police Department.

Resch, Tyler. *Glastenbury: the history of a Vermont ghost town.* Charleston, SC: History Press, 2008.

Rossmo, D. Kim. *Geographic Profiling.* Boca Raton: CRC Press, 2000.

Rudd, Malcolm Day. *An Historical Sketch of Salisbury*. New York, 1899.

Saint Albans Daily Messenger.

Salisbury, Rachel E. "The Salisbury Family," *Lippincott's Magazine of Popular Literature and Science*, September 1879.

Smith, Edward H. *Mysteries of the Missing*. New York: The Dial Press, 1927.

Smith, Helen Jensen. "Have You Seen Connie?" *The Torch*: Magazine of Beta Sigma Phi, October 1952.

Spirit of '45. Stamford, Connecticut High School Yearbook.

Springfield Daily News.

Springfield Daily Republican.

Stamford Advocate.

Stock, R. D. & John Zeller. "The Strange Disappearances at Mt. Glastenbury." *Fate Magazine*, July 1957.

Sundance Times.

Syracuse Herald.

Syracuse Standard.

Ticonderoga Sentinel.

Torrington Register.

United States Geological Survey Map, Bennington (Vermont) Quadrangle, January 1898, reprinted 1920.

United States Geological Survey Map, Bennington (Vermont) Quadrangle, 1954.

United States Geological Survey Map, Pittsfield West (Mass.) Quadrangle, 1947.

United States Geological Survey Map, Sharon (Conn.) Quadrangle, 1950.

Vronsky, Peter. *Serial Killers*. New York: Berkley Books, 2004.

Waterbury American.

Waterbury Republican-American.

Wilder, Thornton. *Three Plays*. New York: Harper & Brothers, 1957.

Notes

[1] Edward H. Smith, *Mysteries of the Missing*, xiv-xv.
[2] "Vermont and Billboards," *Hartford Courant*, 25 May 1945, 16.
[3] "Few Vermont Towns Desert Standard Time," *Hartford Courant*, 29 April 1934, C8.
[4] *Bennington College Bulletin* 1946-1947, 8.
[5] "These Girls Do As They Please," *Hartford Courant*, 4 July 1937, E5.
[6] *Spirit of '45*, 72.
[7] Elizabeth Johnson, "My Roommate," Paula Welden Case File #302-303.
[8] Paula Welden Case File #312.
[9] Paula Welden Case File #314.
[10] Paula Welden Case File #316.
[11] Paula Welden Case File #316.
[12] Paula Welden Case File #306.
[13] Paula Welden Case File #318.
[14] Paula Welden Case File #318.
[15] Paula Welden Case File #306.
[16] Paula Welden Case File #309.
[17] Paula Welden Case File #310.
[18] Paula Welden Case File #324.
[19] Paula Welden Case File #324.
[20] Paula Welden Case File #299.
[21] Paula Welden Case File #439.
[22] "Stamford Girl, 18, Disappears at Fashionable Vermont School," *Stamford Advocate*, 3 December 1946, 1, 10.
[23] Paula Welden Case File #437.
[24] Paula Welden Case File #467.
[25] "'I'm Going on Long Trail' Girl Told Louis Knapp," *Bennington Evening Banner*, 5 December 1946, 1.
[26] Report of Almo Franzoni, Paula Welden Case File #436.
[27] Paula Welden Case File #466.
[28] Paula Welden Case File #438.
[29] Report of Lieutenant Robert Rundle, Paula Welden Case File #270.

[30] Paula Welden Case File #291.

[31] "Hunt Vermont Hills for Stamford Girl," *New York Times*, 4 December, 1946, 37.

[32] "Footprints Again a Clue," *Bennington Evening Banner*, 21 December 1946, 1.

[33] "Close to Zero, Winter Hits New England," *Bennington Evening Banner*, 3 December 1946, 1.

[34] "Wide Search Pressed for Welden Girl," *Hartford Courant*, 4 December 1946, 20.

[35] Paula Welden Case File #464.

[36] "Step-by-Step with Clues to Missing Girl," *Bennington Evening Banner*, 6 December 1946, 1, 4.

[37] "Connecticut Girl Sought as Missing," *Hartford Courant*, 3 December 1946, 2.

[38] "Paula Welden Search Ends in Mountain," *Hartford Courant*, 6 December 1946, 2.

[39] "State Detective Almo Franzoni Called in to Help in Search for Missing College Student," *Bennington Evening Banner*, 7 December 1946, 1.

[40] "No Progress in Hunt for Welden Girl," *Hartford Courant*, 7 December, 2.

[41] "State Detective Almo Franzoni Called in to Help in Search for Missing College Student," *Bennington Evening Banner*, 7 December 1946, 1.

[42] "State Detective Almo Franzoni Called in to Help in Search for Missing College Student," *Bennington Evening Banner*, 7 December 1946, 1.

[43] "Blonde Model, Long Island Trio, Two Local Men and Brownish Red Car Latest Leads in Hunt for Missing Welden Girl," *Bennington Evening Banner*, 9 December 1946, 1, 6.

[44] "Foul Play Theory Studied by Police in Welden Case," *Stamford Advocate*, 7 December 1946, 1.

[45] "Would Quiz Three Men in Welden Case," *Hartford Courant*, 9 December 1946, 6.

[46] "Clues Peter Out in Hunt for Student," *Bennington Evening Banner*, 10 December 1946, 1.

[47] "Clues Peter Out in Hunt for Student," *Bennington Evening Banner*, 10 December 1946, 1.

[48] "Police are Baffled as Clues Run Out in Welden Search," *Stamford Advocate*, 10 December 1946, 1, 6.

[49] "Clues Peter Out in Hunt for Student," *Bennington Evening Banner*, 10 December 1946, 8.

[50] "Missing Girl May Be in Canada," *Waterbury American*, 11 December 1946, 1.

[51] "Missing Girl May Be in Canada," *Waterbury American*, 11 December 1946, 1.

[52] "Ask Outside Aid in Search for Missing Paula Welden," *Bennington Evening Banner*, 11 December 1946, 1, 4.

[53] "Welden Case Probe Fails to Progress," *Hartford Courant*, 13 December 1946, 2.

[54] "Detectives Keep Silent about Paula," *Bennington Evening Banner*, 14 December 1946, 1, 5.

[55] "Lieut. Rundle will Question Any Person Who was within Fifty Feet of Paula Welden," *Bennington Evening Banner*, 13 December 1946, 1, 4.

[56] Depending on the police report or news article his name has been spelled both *Gadette* and *Gaudette*. It appears the legal spelling is *Gadette*. When found in a quotation from a printed or written source, the spelling is given as it originally appeared. Elsewhere, *Gadette* is the spelling of choice.

[57] Report of Lieutenant Robert Rundle, Paula Welden Case File #271.

[58] Report of Lieutenant Robert Rundle, Paula Welden Case File #282-283.

[59] Report of Lieutenant Robert Rundle, Paula Welden Case File #288-289.

[60] "Arrest Due Soon in Disappearance of College Girl," *Washington Post*, 15 December 1946, M1.

[61] Report of Lieutenant Robert Rundle, Paula Welden Case File #294-295.

[62] Paula Welden Case File #446.

[63] Paula Welden Case File #454.

[64] Paula Welden Case File #434.

[65] "Welden Ends His Search," *New York Times*, 16 December 1946, 48.

[66] "Thanks Given Local People by Weldens," *Bennington Evening Banner*, 19 December 1946, 1.

[67] "Radio, Press Carry Welden's Appeal to Missing Girl," *Stamford Advocate*. 23 December 1946, 1.

[68] "Death of Paula Welden Probable, Detective Says," *Hartford Courant*, 18 February 1947, 1.

[69] Paula Welden Case File #432.

[70] Paula Welden Case File # 458.

[71] "Officials Lack Knowledge of Lie-Detector Tests," *Bennington Evening Banner*, 10 May 1947, 1.

[72] "Vermont Governor Plans New Search for Paula Welden," *Hartford Courant*, 20 April 1947, 1.

[73] "New Intensive Search for Paula Welden Soon," *Hartford Courant*, 18 May 1947, A19.

[74] "Welden Returns to Stamford, Believes Daughter Lured Away," *Stamford Advocate*, 16 December 1946, 1, 6.

[75] "Nine Groups Search for Paula Welden," *Hartford Courant*, 25 May 1947, 1.

[76] "Searchers Comb Vermont Region for Paula Welden," *Stamford Advocate*, 24 May 1947, 1.

[77] "Paula Welden Not Found as Search Ends," *Hartford Courant*, 26 May 1947, 1.

[78] "Paula Welden Slain, Father Now Believes," *Hartford Courant*, 24 June 1947, 16.

[79] Paula Welden Case File #395.

[80] "Disagreement in Welden Case," *St. Albans Daily Messenger*, 12 September 1952, 1.

[81] "Disappearance of Paula Welden," *Fitchburg Sentinel*, 12 September, 1952, 1.

[82] "Paula Began that Walk Six Years Ago Today," *Bennington Evening Banner*, 1 December 1952, 1, 5.

[83] Report of Lieutenant Robert Rundle, Paula Welden Case File #294-295.

[84] "Disagreement in Welden Case," *St. Albans Daily Messenger*, 12 September 1952, 8.

[85] "Disagreement in Welden Case," *St. Albans Daily Messenger*, 12 September 1952, 8.

[86] Paula Welden Case File #381-383.

[87] "Paula Welden Disappeared 10 Years Ago," *Bennington Evening Banner*, 1 December 1956, 1.

[88] "Paula Welden Missing 12 Years Without Clue," *Hartford Courant*, 2 December 1958, 12.

[89] Guy Ainslee, "A Remarkable Case," 40.

[90] Guy Ainslee, "A Remarkable Case," 40.

[91] Gerald McFarland, *The Counterfeit Man*, 132.

[92] Gerald McFarland, *The Counterfeit Man*, 135.

[93] "No Trace of Middie Rivers is Reported," *Bennington Evening Banner*, 16 November 1945, 1.

[94] "Soldiers Resume Search for Rivers," *Bennington Evening Banner*, 19 November 1945, 1.

[95] "World War I Vet is Still Missing," *Bennington Evening Banner*, 8 December 1949, 1.

[96] "Rain-Soaked Posse Hunts White Chapel Woods for 8 Year Old Paul Jepson," *Bennington Evening Banner*, 13 October 1950, 1, 4.

[97] "Rain-Soaked Posse Hunts White Chapel Woods for 8 Year Old Paul Jepson," *Bennington Evening Banner*, 13 October 1950, 1, 4.

[98] "Coast Guard Sends Plane to Join Search for Missing Paul Jepson," *Bennington Evening Banner*, 14 October 1950, 1.

[99] "Missing Jepson Youngster Makes Fourth Disappearance of Local Persons in 5 Years." *Bennington Evening Banner*, 24 October 1950, 1.

[100] "Missing Jepson Youngster Makes Fourth Disappearance of Local Persons in 5 Years." *Bennington Evening Banner*, 24 October 1950, 1.

[101] "Combing Somerset Reservoir Woods for Mrs. Freida Langer; Disappeared Late Saturday," *Bennington Evening Banner*, 30 October 1950, 1, 4.

[102] "Elsner Found in Somerset in Time to Give Testimony at Inquest in Brattleboro," *Bennington Evening Banner*, 4 November 1950, 1.

[103] "Officials, Woods Crew and Relatives Head into Rain-Soaked Woods Today, *Bennington Evening Banner*, 3 November 1950, 1.

[104] "Elsner, Cousin of Mrs. Langer, Missing," *Bennington Evening Banner*, 3 November, 1950, 1.

[105] "Langer, Elsner Abandon Hope of Finding Missing Woman; Return Home," *Bennington Evening Banner*, 13 November 1950, 1, 4.

[106] "Langer, Elsner Take Truth Test," *Brattleboro Reformer*, 6 November 1950, 1.

[107] " 'Get Out and Find that Body' Order Given in Langer Case; Ask 400 Troops for Search," *Bennington Evening Banner*, 7 November 1950, 1.

[108] "Two Stamford Fishermen Share Reward for Finding Body of Mrs. Langer on Bank of Stream Below Somerset Dam," *Bennington Evening Banner*, 14 May 1951, 1, 4.

[109] "Elsner, Cousin of Mrs. Langer Missing," *Bennington Evening Banner*, 3 November 1950, 1, 3.

[110] "Two Stamford Fishermen Share Reward for Finding Body of Mrs. Langer on Bank of Stream Below Somerset Dam," *Bennington Evening Banner*, 14 May 1951, 1, 4.

[111] "Two Stamford Fishermen Share Reward for Finding Body of Mrs. Langer on Bank of Stream Below Somerset Dam," *Bennington Evening Banner*, 14 May 1951, 1, 4.

[112] "White Hart Inn Opened by Fox Hunt," *Hartford Courant*, 22 December 1929, 1.

[113] "Dr. Spoth Gets 10 to 15 Years," *Hartford Courant*, 14 May 1924, 1.

[114] "Malicious Killing of Cow Charged in Salisbury Case," *Hartford Courant*, 13 October 1949, 3.

[115] Rev. Joseph W. Crossman, *New Year's Discourse delivered at Salisbury*, 1803, 12.

[116] Rachel E Salisbury, "The Salisbury Family," *Lippincott's Magazine of Popular Literature and Science*, September 1879, 380.

[117] Malcolm Day Rudd, *An Historical Sketch of Salisbury*, 1899.

[118] "Camp Sloane Officials Enter Not Guilty Pleas," *Hartford Courant*, 25 July 1940, 6.

[119] "Youth Drowns in Pond at Lakeville," *Waterbury Republican*, 19 June 1942, 3.

[120] It appears this was an event at Camp Sloane that happened to coincide with the Annual Lakeville Horse Show scheduled to start that day.

[121] Helen Jensen Smith, "Have You Seen Connie?" *The Torch*, October 1952.

[122] Connie Smith Case File, Report by Detective Sgt. William Menser, 17 July 1952.

[123] "Gov. Lodge Felicitates State Police," *Hartford Courant*, 1 July 1953, 24.

[124] "Police Plane Joins Search for Girl, 10," *Waterbury American*, 18 July 1952, 3.

[125] "After 32 Years, Father's Search Continues for Missing Girl," *Hartford Courant*, 22 November 1984, G7.

[126] "Police Plane Joins Search for Girl, 10," *Waterbury American*, 18 July 1952, 3.

[127] Connie Smith Case File, Report by Detective Sgt. William N. Menser, 18 July 1952, 1.

[128] "Connie Smith Now Missing Two Years," Waterbury Republican, 15 July 1954, 1.

[129] Connie Smith Case File, Report by Officer Victor J. Keilty, 17 July 1952, 1.

[130] "Police Plane Joins Search for Girl, 10," *Waterbury American*, 18 July 1952, 3.

[131] "A Camper Walks Away, Picks Daisies and Vanishes," *Hartford Courant*, 16 July 2000, A-1.

[132] "Smith Girl Searchers Take to Air," *Hartford Courant*, 19 July 1952, 8.

[133] "Police File Still Active in 10-Year Mystery," *Hartford Courant*, 15 July 1962, 4B3.

[134] "Police to Await New Lead in Hunt for Connie Smith," *Hartford Courant*, 5 August 1952, 5.

[135] "Mother of Missing Girl Appeals to State Hunters," *Hartford Courant*, 29 November 1952, 1.

[136] Connie Smith Case File, Report by Officer Leo Turcotte, 29 November 1952, 1.

[137] "'Talking' Horse Credited with Lead in Finding Body," *Hartford Courant*, 8 December 1952, 1.

[138] "Search for Connie Smith Turns to Los Angeles" *Hartford Courant*, 10 April 1953, 1.

[139] "Confession Doubted in Connie Smith Case," *Hartford Courant*, 8 April 1953, 1.

[140] "Confession Doubted in Connie Smith Case," *Hartford Courant*, 8 April 1953, 2.

[141] "Confession Doubted in Connie Smith Case," *Hartford Courant*, 8 April 1953, 2.

[142] "Smith Girl's 'Murder' is Hoax, Man Admits," *Hartford Courant*, 9 April 1953, 1.

[143] "Whatever Happened to Connie?," *Hartford Courant*, 16 July 1967, 2F.

[144] Classified Ad, *Waterbury Republican*, 9 May 1957, 46.

[145] Connie Smith Case File, Report by Officer Charles Sedar, 10 September 1952, 1.

[146] "Connie Smith Once Object of Nation-Wide Search," *Waterbury Sunday Republican*, 19 April 1959, 12.

[147] "City Woman Found Dead in Wolcott; Foul Play Possible," *Waterbury Republican*, 22 April 1957, 1.

[148] "Funeral Set Today for Mrs. Martin," *Waterbury Republican*, 24 April 1957, 2.

[149] "Officials Doubt Girl in Picture is Connie Smith," *Hartford Courant*, 4 August, 1954, 9C.

[150] "License Plate, Scar Etched in Memory," *Waterbury Republican-American*, 7 September 2002, 1 & 4.

[151] "Search for Connie Smith Turns to Los Angeles Area," *Hartford Courant*, 10 April, 1953, 1, 2.

[152] "Confession Doubted in Connie Smith Case," *Hartford Courant*, 8 April 1953, 1.

[153] "Trooper Hopes 22-Year Mystery will be Solved," *Hartford Courant*, 14 July 1974, 31A.

[154] "Girl Camper's Disappearance Likened to Welden Mystery," *Berkshire Evening Eagle*, 31 July 1952, 2.

[155] "Confession Doubted in Connie Smith Case," *Hartford Courant*, 8 April 1953, 1.

[156] "Special Short Trip No. 10, Automobile Club of Hartford," *Hartford Courant*, 7 October 1934, C7.

[157] John Disturnell, *The Traveler's Guide to the Hudson River*, 42.

[158] Newspapers differed on this; some reporting Katherine as being 22, 23 or 24 years old.

[159] "Missing for Ten Days," *New York Times*, 18 September, 1887.

[160] "A Girl's Freak," *The* (Fresno) *Daily Republican*, 8 October 1887, 2.

[161] "Mystery Still Shrouds Girl's Disappearance," *Chatham Courier*, 9 April 1936, 1.

[162] "Reward is Offered in Search for Miss Hull," *Syracuse Herald*, 10 August 1936.

[163] "Doubts that Skull Found near Saranac is that of Daughter," *Ticonderoga Sentinel*, 20 January 1944, 1.

[164] "Widen Search for Missing Girl; Last Seen at Lebanon Springs," Albany *Times Union*, 11 April 1936, 2.

[165] "Searchers Still Minus Clues on Missing Girl," Albany *Times Union*, 6 April 1936, 2.

[166] "Police Extend Hunt for Girl Missing 3 Days," Albany *Times Union*, 5 April 1936, 8-B.

[167] "Mystery Woman who Gave Tip on Hull Girl is Pledged Immunity," *Syracuse Herald*, 19 April 1936, 2-C & 6-C.

[168] "Detectives to Continue Probe of Hancock Mountain," *Springfield Republican*, 23 April 1943, 2-D.

[169] "Detectives to Continue Probe of Hancock Mountain," *Springfield Republican*, 23 April, 1944, 2D.

[170] Interview with West Mountain hunter James Scace.

[171] "Skull and Bones Start Search for Missing Persons," *Hudson Daily Star*, 13 December 1943, 3.

[172] "Skull and Bones Start Search for Missing Persons," *Hudson Daily Star*, 13 December 1943, 3.

[173] Correspondence with James Scace, 17 December 2007.

[174] Massachusetts State Police Laboratory Logbook Entry, 11 December 1943.

[175] "Detectives to Continue Probe of Hancock Mountain," *Springfield Republican*, 23 April 1944, 2D.

[176] "Doubts that Skull Found near Saranac is that of Daughter," *Ticonderoga Sentinel*, 20 January 1944, 1.

[177] "FBI Director Asks Action to Control Sex Offenders," *Hartford Courant*, 24 February 1955, 19A.

[178] Eric W. Hickey, *Serial Murderers and Their Victims*.

[179] "Piracy and Murder – The Coolie Trade," *New York Times*, 21 July 1853.

[180] D. Kim Rossmo, *Geographic Profiling*, 140-141.

[181] D. Kim Rossmo, *Geographic Profiling*, 140-141.

[182] Peter Vronsky, *Serial Killers*, 100-101.

[183] Peter Vronsky, *Serial Killers*, 101.

[184] D. Kim Rossmo, *Geographic Profiling*, 33.

[185] Peter Vronsky, *Serial Killers*, 361.

[186] D. Kim Rossmo, *Geographic Profiling*, 213.

[187] Quoted in D. Kim Rossmo, *Geographic Profiling*, 129.

[188] "My Fascination with the Welden Case," *Bennington Banner*, 6 December 1996, 10.

[189] "The Strange Ways of Amnesia," *Hartford Courant*, 1 January 1933, E3.

[190] "Paula Welden Slain, Father Now Believes," *Hartford Courant*, 24 June 1947, 16.

[191] "What Happened to Paula Welden," *Hartford Courant*, 4 December 1966, 20A.

[192] "Father's Search has not Ended," *Lakeville Journal*, 15 November 1984, 1.

[193] "Father's Search has not Ended," *Lakeville Journal*, 15 November 1984, 1.

[194] "Camper's Fate a 57-year-old Mystery," *Republican-American*, 11 May 2009.

[195] D. Kim Rossmo, *Geographic Profiling*, 130.